Simple Handmade Storage

Simple Handmade Storage

Philip and Kate Haxell

23 step-by-step weekend projects

LAUREL GLEN

San Diego, California

Contents

For our seven brothers,
    including those that can't hammer a nail in straight

Laurel Glen Publishing
An imprint of the Advantage Publishers Group
5880 Oberlin Drive, San Diego, CA 92121-4794
www.laurelglenbooks.com

All notations of errors or omissions should be addressed to Laurel Glen Publishing, Editorial Department, at the above address. All other correspondence (author inquiries, permissions, and rights) concerning the content of this book should be addressed to Cico Books Ltd, 32 Great Sutton Street, London, EC1V 0NB, UK.

Library of Congress Cataloging-in-Publication Data
Haxell, Philip.
  Simple handmade storage: 23 step-by-step weekend projects/Philip and Kate Haxell.
    p. cm.
  ISBN 1-59223-150-0
    1. Cabinetwork—Amateurs' manuals. 2. Storage in the home—Amateurs' manuals.
    3. Shelving (Furniture)—Amateurs' manuals. I. Haxell, Kate. II. Title.

TT197.H367 2004
684.1'6—dc22

                                    2003062497

Editor: Kate Haxell; designer: Roger Daniels; photographers: Lucinda Symons and Brian Hatton; stylist: Denise Brock; Illustrations: Philip Haxell
Printed in Singapore
1 2 3 4 5 08 07 06 05 04

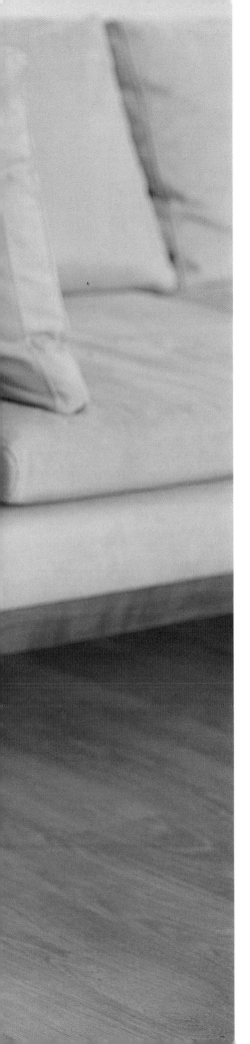

Introduction

Having moved home into an older property, which had almost nothing in the way of built-in storage, we quickly became painfully aware of the quantity of our possessions, and the lack of efficient storage we had to keep them in. After living among the clutter for a few months, the need to sort it all out and give everything a home of its own became pressing.

We investigated store-bought storage solutions, and found that while many of them were well-made and practical, they just weren't quite right for the items we wanted to store, or for the space we had available. We consulted friends, and found that without exception they all had similar storage problems.

The obvious answer was to build our own storage—and as soon as we mentioned it, storage for our friends, too. So within this book you will find 23 clever, efficient and easy-to-make storage solutions for all kinds of items, from bed linen to books to the television. Different pieces were designed to suit different homes and spaces, there are a range of decorative styles, from country to contemporary. Many pieces have additional advice on altering the dimensions to fit your space, and on customizing the finish to suit your taste.

Some projects are very simple indeed and can be tackled by a complete woodworking novice. Others are a bit more complex, but none require any special woodworking skills, just care and attention to detail when measuring, cutting and fixing.

Always read all the steps of a project through carefully before you begin, and consult the relevant techniques where necessary. If you have never tried a particular technique before, practice it first on a scrap piece of wood before you start the project.

Each project lists the tools needed to complete it, and most need only the basics. Check the Toolbox on page 108, and if you do decide to get a new tool, especially if it is an expensive one, try to borrow or hire one first to ensure that you are happy using it before you buy. Always, always follow a manufacturer's operating instructions when using a tool—handling it wrongly or skipping a safety instruction can lead to trouble.

We hope that you find these projects useful, and that soon you, too, will have a purpose-built home for everything you need to store.

PHILIP AND KATE HAXELL

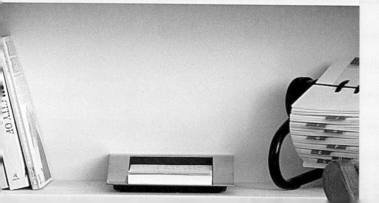

The Basics

The vast majority of storage furniture is a variation on one of three basic pieces: a shelving unit, a box, or a cupboard. This chapter shows you how to make these three staple pieces, which will be used in other projects.

Basic Bookcase

Books always occupy far more space than seems reasonable, and most bookcases are too deep and the shelves too widely spaced to accommodate the maximum number of books in the minimum amount of space. The secret to storing books efficiently is simple; make the bookcase shelves exactly the right size for the standard book formats. This allows you to store books of various heights on different shelves in the bookcase. If you wish, you can include higher shelves for knickknacks or stereo equipment and lower shelves for CDs.

YOU WILL NEED

MDF

Base and top
- Two pieces 35 x 6½ x ¾ in.

Sides
- Two pieces 73½ x 6½ x ¾ in.

Plinth
- One piece 33½ x 7½ x ¾ in.

Shelves
- Seven pieces 33½ x 6½ x ¾ in.

Back
- One piece 75 x 35 x ¼ in.

- Drill
- ³⁄₁₆ in. and ⅛ in. drill bits
- Countersink bit
- Tape measure
- Pencil
- Wood glue
- Screwdriver

Screws
- 42: 1³⁄₈ in.
- 24: 1 in.

- Try square
- Filling knife
- Filler
- Sanding block
- 120-grit sandpaper
- Paintbrush
- Primer
- Satin paint

1 Predrill and countersink ³⁄₁₆ in. holes in the base and top pieces, ½ in. in from the edge (see Drilling and Countersinking, page 12). On the short sides, position one hole 2 in. from each end. On one long side of the base piece only, position one hole 2¾ in. from each end, with one more hole spaced centrally between them.

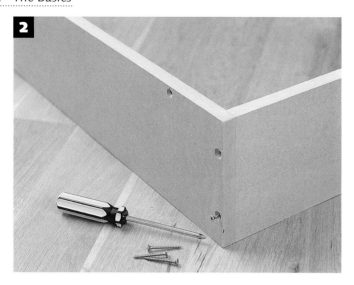

2 Butt one short edge of a side piece against one short end of the base, ensuring that the drilled long side of the base is at the front. Using a ⅛ in. drill bit, drill pilot holes through the predrilled holes in the base piece into the edges of the side pieces. Glue and screw the two pieces together, driving 1⅜ in. screws through the predrilled holes into the pilot holes (see Joining Two Pieces with Screws, page 13). Attach the other side piece to the other end of the base piece in the same way. Attach the top piece to the other ends of the side pieces in the same way to make a rectangular frame.

DRILLING AND COUNTERSINKING

1 Mark the point at which you want to drill the hole with an X. Hold the drill perpendicular to the surface, so that you are not drilling at an angle. Start drilling slowly to allow the drill bit to bite into the wood in the right spot. Speed up and put your weight behind the drill to drill right through the wood.

2 Where it is important that the screw holes are not visible, countersink the hole. This allows the screw head to sit below the surface of the wood, and the hole can later be filled (see Finishing Techniques, page 110). Fit the countersink bit into the drill and push it into the drilled hole. Drill a hole with sloped sides deep enough for the screw head to fit into.

When you are countersinking side pieces for a project, take care to work on opposite faces of the wood to produce right- and left-hand pieces with the countersinking on the outer faces.

If you are attaching the edge of a piece of wood to the flat surface of another piece through a predrilled hole, it is best to drill a pilot hole to avoid the edge of the wood splitting. Position the two pieces of wood together correctly, then, using a ⅛ in. drill bit, drill a tiny hole right through the predrilled hole in the flat piece, into the edge of the other piece. Drill the hole to the approximate depth of the screw you are going to use.

3 To drill a larger hole you need to use a spade bit. Mark the position of the hole as in Step 1. Place the point of the spade bit on the mark and drill slowly through the wood. For a neat finish, stop drilling just as the point of the bit appears on the other side. Turn the wood over, place the point of the bit in the hole, and finish drilling from this side.

4 Really big holes are drilled with a hole saw. Mark the position of the hole as in Step 1. Place the point of the hole saw on the mark and drill slowly through the wood. You will find it easier to clamp the piece of wood in place before you start, as the friction from the saw can cause it to spin around. For a neat finish, stop drilling just as the point of the bit appears on the other side. Turn the wood over, place the point of the bit in the hole, and finish drilling from this side. A hole saw will become blunt if it gets too hot, so don't apply a lot of pressure when drilling—you will hear the drill slow down if you are pressing too hard—and back off intermittently to allow the cutter to cool down. Always remove the cutout piece of wood from the hole saw before cutting another hole.

JOINING TWO PIECES WITH SCREWS

1 Follow the instructions on the glue you buy, as different types vary. Apply glue to one or both of the surfaces to be joined (this may vary depending on the type of glue). Push the pieces together.

2 Check that you have the correct size of screw; it should be long enough to go right through the top piece of wood with at least half of it going into the bottom piece. It should not be too long or it will go right through both pieces. Use a screwdriver to drive the screw through the predrilled hole and into the pilot hole in the bottom piece of wood. Immediately wipe away any excess glue with a damp cloth.

   In this book we have used ³⁄₁₆ in. thick, countersink screws with crossheads, unless otherwise stated.

3 Mark the height of the plinth on both sides of the bookcase with a pencil line, and draw another parallel line ½ in. above that line (see Using a Try Square, below). Predrill and countersink two holes, each 2 in. in from the edge, on the higher line. Fit

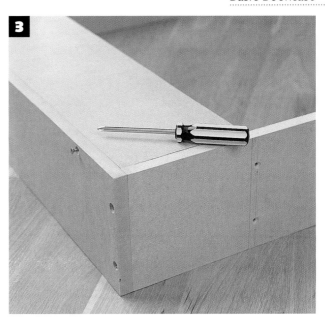

the plinth into the bookcase, ensuring that it is flat against the fronts of the sides. Drill pilot holes through the predrilled holes in the base piece into the edge of the plinth. Glue and screw the pieces together, driving 1³⁄₈ in. screws through the predrilled holes into the pilot holes.

USING A TRY SQUARE

1 A try square makes drawing parallel lines easy. Push the top of the try square against the edge of the piece you are working on and slide it along to the marked point. Draw a pencil line along the metal edge, then slide the try square the required distance and draw another line.

2 When fitting shelves, always use a try square to check that they are at right-angles to the back and sides, and therefore level. Simply aligning them with drilled holes is not enough. Put the shelf in place, then push the try square tightly up against the shelf and the back. One end of the try square must lie flat along the shelf and the other end flat along the back. Repeat the procedure on the sides.

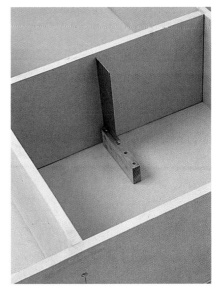

4 Predrill and countersink three holes in the long side of one shelf, ½ in. in from the edge. Position one hole 2¾ in. from each end, with one more hole spaced centrally between them. Drill pilot holes through the predrilled holes in the shelf and side pieces into the edge of the plinth and shelf. Glue and screw the pieces together, driving 1⅜ in. screws through the predrilled holes into the pilot holes.

5 Predrill and countersink twenty-four holes in the back piece, ½ in. in from the edge. On the long sides, position one hole 2 in. from each end, with five more holes spaced evenly between them. On the short sides, position one hole 2 in. from each end, with three more spaced evenly between them. Lay the frame facedown and position the back piece over it, aligning all edges. Drill pilot

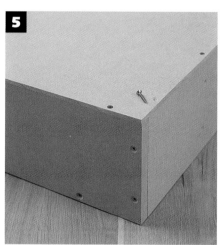

holes through the predrilled holes in the back piece into the edges of the side, top, and base pieces. Glue and screw the pieces together, driving 1 in. screws through the predrilled holes into the pilot holes.

6 Measure and mark the height of the second shelf up on the sides of the bookcase with a pencil line. Draw another line ½ in. above that line and predrill and countersink holes on the higher line, as in Step 3. Fit the shelf in place, aligning it with the drilled holes and using a try square to check that it is straight and at right-angles to the back. Drill pilot holes, glue, and screw the second shelf to the

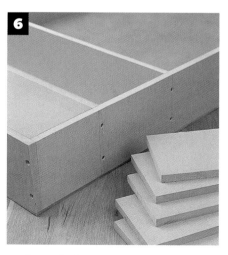

sides of the bookcase, driving 1⅜ in. screws through the predrilled holes into the pilot holes. Repeat the process until all the shelves are in place. Fill all screw holes, sand the whole bookcase, and prime it, then paint it with two coats of satin paint (see Finishing Techniques, page 110).

customizing
THE BOOKCASE

This basic bookcase can be altered to almost any height and width, and the shelves spaced to accommodate whatever you want to store. If you are working with ¾ in. thick MDF for the shelves, and you want to make the bookcase more than 39 in. wide, measure and mark the positions of the shelves on the back of the bookcase. Predrill, countersink, and pilot-drill holes approximately every 12 in., and drive screws through the back into the edges of the shelves, or they will sag in the middle over time.

To adjust the height of the bookcase, figure out how many shelves you want and the spacing between them. Add the spaces and the thicknesses of the shelves together. Add the height of the plinth to this sum to give the length of the side pieces. Add the thickness of the top and base to this figure to give the final height of the bookcase.

For a really professional-looking finish, make the plinth exactly the same height as the baseboard the bookcase will stand against.

This combination of bookcase and cupboards provides plentiful, flexible storage. The cupboards are built with a plinth base, following the principle of the Basic Bookcase, but with very short sides and doors.

The bookcase is built in the same way as the Basic Bookcase, but without a base, plinth, or bottom shelf.

Stand the bookcase on top of the cupboard and screw up through the top of the cupboard into the ends of the sides and central struts to hold the two elements together. To make it really stable, a large bookcase should also be fastened to the wall through the back (see Hanging Items on Walls, page 113).

Basic Blanket Box

One of the simplest and most useful pieces of storage you can make is this basic blanket box. It can be made in almost any dimension to fit particular spaces and will happily hold anything you want to put in it. The angled lid makes it easier to find things in it, and the flat top allows it to serve as a table when it is closed.

YOU WILL NEED

MDF

Sides

• Two pieces 18⅝ x 18½ x ⅝ in.

Base

• One piece 39¼ x 19¾ x ⅝ in.

Lid

• One piece 39¼ x 19¾ x ⅝ in.
• One piece 39¼ x 7¼ x ⅝ in.
• One piece 39¼ x 1⅜ x ⅝ in.

Back

• One piece 39¼ x 17⅛ x ⅝ in.

Front

• One piece 39¼ x 11¼ x ⅝ in.

Feet

• Four pieces 2 x 2 x ⅝ in.

• Tape measure
• Pencil
• Jigsaw
• Drill
• ³⁄₁₆ in. and ⅛ in. drill bits
• Countersink bit
• Wood glue
• Screwdriver

Screws

• 50: 1⅜ in.
• 4: 1 in.
• 12: ½ in.
• 2: ⅝ in.

• Two 3 in. butt hinges
• Mallet
• Chisel
• 24 in. long chain
• 2 washers
• Filling knife
• Filler
• Sanding block
• 120-grit sandpaper
• Paintbrush
• Primer
• Satin paint

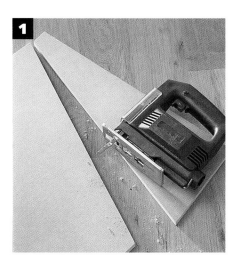

1 On one long side of both side pieces, measure up 11¼ in. and make a pencil mark. On the opposite side, measure up 17⅛ in. and make another pencil mark. Join the two marks with a pencil line. Using a jigsaw, cut accurately along the line (see Cutting with a Jigsaw, below). The smaller pieces are the sides of the lid and the larger pieces are the sides of the box.

2 Predrill and countersink the following ³⁄₁₆ in. holes, ¼ in. in from the edge of the relevant pieces of MDF (see Drilling and Countersinking, page 12).

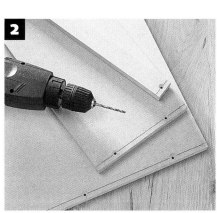

In the base and large lid (top) pieces, drill five holes on each long side. Position one hole 2⅜ in. from each end, with three more holes spaced evenly between them. On the short sides drill three holes, one 2⅜ in. in from each corner, with one more hole centrally between them.

In the middle-sized lid (front) piece, drill two holes on each short side. Position one hole 2 in. in from each corner.

In the small lid (back) piece, drill one hole on each short side. Position the hole centrally.

In the back piece, drill three holes on each short side. Position one hole 2⅜ in. in from each corner, with one more hole between them.

In the front piece, drill three holes on each short side. Position one hole 2⅜ in. in from each corner, with one more hole between them.

CUTTING WITH A JIGSAW

The key to accurate cutting is to ensure that the surface you are working on is firmly secured and to take your time. Guide the blade along the line you have drawn, and if you go off course, don't panic; simply stop and restart in the right direction. Minor mistakes can be smoothed away with sandpaper. For the best results, the blade should be sharp.

If you find it difficult to cut straight lines with a jigsaw, consider getting the wood cut professionally. Most home improvement stores and lumber yards offer a cutting service if you buy the wood from them.

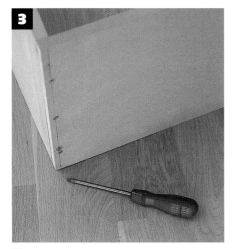

3 Start by assembling the box. Butt one short edge of a side piece up to one end of the front piece. Using a ⅛ in. drill bit, drill pilot holes through the predrilled holes in the front piece into the edges of the side piece. Glue and screw the two pieces together, driving 1⅜ in. screws through the predrilled holes into the pilot holes (see Joining Two Pieces with Screws, page 13).

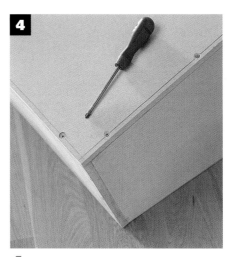

4 Turn the pieces upside down and lay the base piece over them. Drill pilot holes through the predrilled holes in the base into the edges of the front and side pieces. Glue and screw the two pieces together, driving 1⅜ in. screws through the predrilled holes into the pilot holes.

5 Fix the other side piece in place, drilling, gluing, and screwing it as in Step 2.

6 Butt the back piece up to the long edges of the sides. Drill pilot holes through the predrilled holes in the back into the edges of the sides. Glue and screw the pieces together using 1⅜ in. screws.

7 Make up the lid in the same order and using the same methods. Attach the front to the short edge of one side piece, then attach the lid top to those pieces. Attach the other side piece and finally the lid back. Use 1⅜ in. screws throughout.

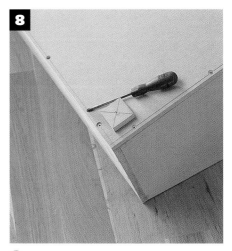

8 Predrill and countersink a 3⁄16 in. hole through the center of each foot. Mark points on the base 2 in. from each side of the corners. Position a foot centrally on each marked point and glue and screw them to the base, driving 1 in. screws through the predrilled holes in the feet into the base.

9 Attach the lid to the box using butt hinges and ½ in. screws (see Rabbeting a Butt Hinge, right). Lay one hinge 6 in. from each end, with the knuckle of the hinge along the joint between the lid and the

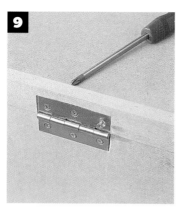

box. Attach one end of the chain to the inside of one lid side piece, 6 in. from the front. Position the link of the chain in the right spot, lay the washer over it, and drive a ⅝ in. screw through the washer and link into the lid. Attach the other end of the chain to the inside of the adjacent box side piece, 8½ in. from the front, in the same way. Fill all screw holes, sand the whole bookcase, and prime it, then paint it with two coats of satin paint (see Finishing Techniques, page 110).

In a small bedroom the box can double as an occasional—or even bedside—table, as well as provide storage.

RABBETING A BUTT HINGE

1 Lay the two pieces to be hinged together next to one another in the right position. Lay a hinge in place, with the knuckle of the hinge uppermost and along the joint between the two pieces. Draw right around the hinge.

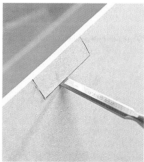

2 Remove the hinges and the part of the piece of furniture that will move on the hinge. Working on the static part of the piece, place the chisel on the pencil line with the sloping edge facing into the drawn shape. Using the mallet, tap the chisel into the MDF right around the line. Chisel down to the depth of the flat metal part of the hinge.

3 Working from the edge of the box, tap the chisel into the MDF at the depth at which you chiseled down in Step 2. Work along the edge and then tap the chisel in a little further until the rectangle of MDF lifts off to create a rabbet. Repeat the process on the other drawn hinge shape on the moving part of the piece.

4 Reposition the two pieces next to one another. Fit the hinges into the chiseled-out rabbets. Drill pilot holes through each hole in the hinge, then screw the hinges in place, driving ½ in. screws into the pilot holes.

Basic Cupboard

Simple and quick to make, this versatile cupboard can be adapted to suit any room. Here it is a kitchen cupboard, but it would be equally useful in a bedroom, bathroom, or office. It is also a perfect project for a novice woodworker to try.

1 Predrill and countersink the following ¾₁₆ in. holes (see Drilling and Countersinking, page 12).

In the top and base pieces, drill five holes along each long side, ¼ in. in from the edge. Position one hole 2¼ in. from each end, with three more spaced evenly between them.

On each side piece, draw lines right across the outside, 10¾ in. down from the top edge and up from the bottom edge. Drill three holes on these lines, positioning one hole 2¼ in. from the back edge, and one hole 3⅛ in. from the front edge, with one hole centrally between them.

In the back piece, drill holes along each side, ¼ in. in from the edge. Position one hole 2¼ in. from each corner. On the short sides, position one hole centrally between them; on the long sides, position three more holes spaced evenly between them.

2 Lay one side piece flat. Butt one short edge of a side piece against a predrilled end of the top piece. Using a ⅛ in. drill bit, drill pilot holes through the predrilled holes in the top piece into the edges of the side piece. Glue and screw the two pieces together, driving 1⅜ in. screws through the predrilled holes into the pilot holes (see Joining Two Pieces with Screws, page 13).

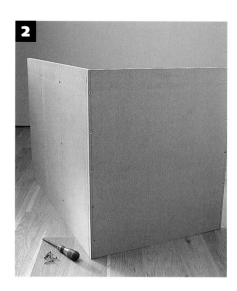

customizing

THE CUPBOARD

This is a very simple project to customize, as you simply alter the height and depth of the cupboard to suit the space available. The side pieces are always the same size, as are the top and base pieces and the back and door pieces, though the back is usually made out of thinner wood to keep the weight down. You can install as many or as few shelves as you wish. Decide on the positions you would like the shelves to be in, then measure and mark the side pieces and predrill holes, as in Step 1.

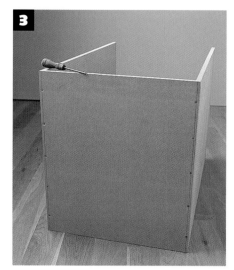

3 Glue and screw the remaining side piece to the other side of the top, as in Step 2.

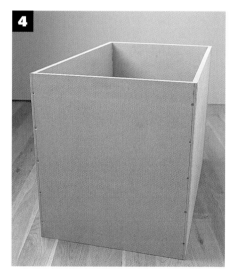

4 Butt the base piece up to the ends of the sides. Drill pilot holes through the predrilled holes in the base piece into the edges of the side pieces. Glue and screw the pieces together, driving 1⅜ in. screws through the predrilled holes into the pilot holes.

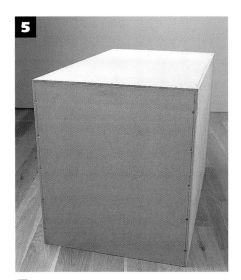

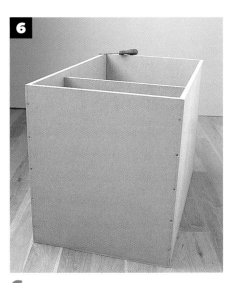

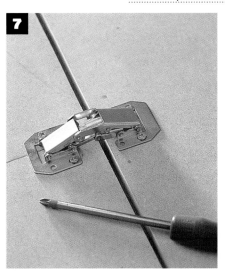

5 Lay the back piece over the frame, aligning the edges carefully. Drill pilot holes through the predrilled holes in the back piece into the edges of the sides, top, and base. Glue and screw the back in place, driving 1 in. screws through the predrilled holes into the pilot holes.

6 Fit a shelf in position, aligning it with opposite rows of predrilled holes in the sides. Drill pilot holes as before, and glue and screw the shelf in place using 1⅜ in. screws. Fit the other shelf in the same way. Attach the feet to the base of the cupboard following Step 8 of Basic Blanket Box (see page 18), and using 1 in. screws.

7 Hang the door using lay-on hinges and ½ in. screws (see Hanging a Door Using Lay-on Hinges, below). Fill all screw holes, sand the whole cupboard, and prime it, then paint it with two coats of satin paint (see Finishing Techniques, page 110). Attach the handle to the door.

HANGING A DOOR USING LAY-ON HINGES

1 Draw a horizontal line on the back of the door where the hinge will lie; approximately 5 in. from the top and bottom of the door is usually right. Check that when the hinge is attached at the marked position, it won't get in the way of the internal shelves. Close the hinge and place it centrally on the line. Balance a scrap piece of wood—the same thickness as the body of the cupboard—on edge and flush with the edge of the door. Push the hinge up to the scrap piece of wood. Drill pilot holes and screw one end of the hinge to the door through the long slots only,

using ½ in. screws. Push the free end of the hinge up to the scrap piece of wood and make pencil marks through the long slots onto the scrap wood. Measure the distances from the edge of the scrap wood to the marked points.

2 Lay the body of the piece on the side you want the hinges to be on. Lay the door facedown on the floor next to it and align the tops and bottoms of the door and the body. Using the measurements established in Step 1, mark the hinge fixing points on the body. Ensure that the marks are in line with the holes in the hinge.

3 Open the hinge and position the holes over the marked points on the body. Pilot-drill and screw the hinge to the body through the long slots only, using ½ in. screws. Stand the cupboard up and open, and close the door to ensure that it is hanging properly. If necessary, slide the ends of the hinges along on the screws in the slots until it is adjusted correctly. When the door is moving freely and sitting flush to the cupboard when closed, drill pilot holes through the small holes in the ends of the hinges, and drive ½ in. screws into the pilot holes.

The Hallway

This is a difficult room, as it is nearly always too small for the clutter it has to contain. Custom-designed storage can make your hallway welcoming to visitors rather than looking like a dumping ground.

Letter Rack

Mail can quickly build up into messy piles in a hallway, but this letter rack makes it neat. There is a letter holder for each member of the family and a hook for each person's keys. The whole rack hangs on the wall and takes up very little space in even the narrowest hallway.

YOU WILL NEED

MDF

backboard
- One piece 47¼ x 17 x ½ in.

Letter holders
- Four pieces 8¾ x 7⅛ x ¼ in.
- Four pieces 6¼ x 2 x ½ in.

- Template on page 114
- Jigsaw
- Drill
- ³⁄₁₆ in. and ⅛ in. drill bits
- Countersink bit
- Sanding block
- 80-grit sandpaper
- 120-grit sandpaper
- Tape measure
- Pencil
- Ruler
- Wood glue
- Staple gun
- ⅝ in. staples
- Screwdriver

Screws
- 8: 1¼ in.
- 8: ¾ in.
- 4: suitable for wall fixings, with domed caps

- 6 hooks
- Filling knife
- Filler
- Paintbrush
- Primer
- Satin paint
- Suitable wall fixings

1 Enlarge the template by 500 percent and transfer it onto the backboard piece of MDF, transferring all the marks (see Template Techniques, page 112). Using a jigsaw, cut out the shape (see Cutting with a Jigsaw, page 17). Predrill the ³⁄₁₆ in. holes in each corner. Predrill and countersink on the back the remaining ³⁄₁₆ in. holes (see Drilling and Countersinking, page 12). Round off the front edge all around with 80-grit sandpaper, then smooth it with 120-grit sandpaper (see Finishing Techniques, page 110). If you have a router, you can use a rounding-over bit to rout a curve around the edge instead, following Step 1 of Mirror with Trays (see page 76).

2 On one long (bottom) side of each of the four larger (front) letter holder pieces, make a pencil mark ½ in. in from each edge. Draw sloping pencil lines from these marks up to the corners on the other long (top) side. Using a jigsaw, cut along these lines.

3 Round off the front edge of the long, straight (top) side, and both the corners on this side. Round off the front edge of the short, straight (bottom) side.

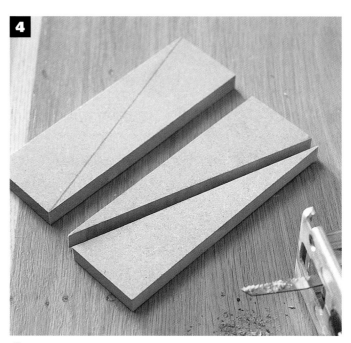

4 Draw a diagonal line across each of the smaller letter holder pieces. Using a jigsaw, cut along these lines to make eight triangles.

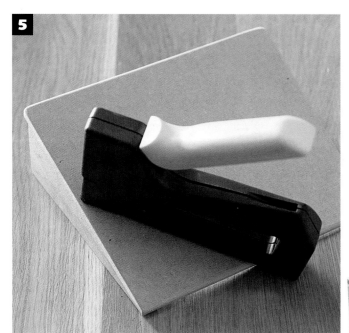

5 Position the sloping edge of a triangle against each sloping side of a front piece, ensuring that they are flush. Align the narrow point of the triangle with the bottom edge of the front piece. Glue and staples the pieces together, firing staples through the front piece into the edges of the triangles (see Joining Two Pieces with Staples, right). Round off the front edges of the sloping sides to match the top and bottom. Make up four holders in this way.

JOINING TWO PIECES WITH STAPLES

A staple gun can be used to join pieces of wood that are too thin to be joined by screws. Spread wood glue over the surfaces to be joined and push them together. Place the head of the staple gun exactly where you want the staple to go, and squeeze the handle hard to fire the staple into the wood. If you are stapling long pieces together, space the staples approximately 2 in. apart.

6 Run a line of glue down each back edge of the triangles on one letter holder. Place the holder on one of the transferred lines on the backboard. Fire two staples through the bottom edge of the holder to tack it to the back. Attach all the holders to the backboard in the same way.

7 Turn the whole rack over and drill a ⅛ in. pilot hole through each predrilled hole in the backboard into the edges of the triangles. Drive screws through the predrilled holes into the pilot holes: drive 1¼ in. screws through the upper holes for each pocket and ¾ in. screws through the lower holes (see Joining Two Pieces with Screws, page 13).

8 Decide where you would like the hooks to be and drill ⅛ in. pilot holes in the backboard for each hook. Fill all staple holes on the front, sand the whole letter rack, and prime it, then paint it with two coats of satin paint (see Finishing Techniques, page 110). Drive the screws supplied through the hooks into the predrilled pilot holes. Use appropriate screws with domed caps and suitable wall fixings to attach the letter rack to the wall, driving the screws through the holes in the corners of the backboard (see Hanging Items on Walls, page 113).

customizing
THE LETTER RACK

If you want a rack with more or fewer letter holders, lengthen or shorten the back piece. As long as the curves flow smoothly and the minimum width is never less than 12 in., the shape of the back piece can be adjusted to any length. To add more holders, transfer the screw hole marks and dotted lines for one of the templated holders to the position where you would like the extra holder to be. You can personalize each holder by painting on the name of the person whose mail it will hold or buying sticky vinyl letters and sticking on the appropriate name.

Below-Stairs Cupboard

The space under a staircase is usually doomed to be a tangled mess of brooms, boots, and cans of paint that have nowhere else to live. This set of sliding cupboards will turn that mess into a tidy, organized home for a multitude of items. It is a major project in terms of scale, but the pieces are simple to make, and the storage you gain is well worth the effort. It is likely that your staircase will vary from the one this cupboard was installed under. Before you start this project, consult the diagrams and instructions on page 116 and follow them to adapt the dimensions to your space.

YOU WILL NEED

MDF

MEDIUM ROLLING CUPBOARD

Sides
- Two pieces
  $34^3/_{16}$ x $14^3/_{16}$ x $5/_8$ in.

Fascia
- One piece
  $38^{11}/_{16}$ x $15^5/_8$ x $3/_8$ in.

Back
- One piece
  $23^{13}/_{16}$ x $21^7/_{16}$ x $3/_8$ in.

Top
- One piece
  $21^7/_{16}$ x $18^{15}/_{16}$ x $5/_8$ in.

Base
- One piece
  $21^7/_{16}$ x $14^3/_{16}$ x $3/_4$ in.

Shelf
- One piece
  $20^3/_{16}$ x $14^3/_{16}$ x $3/_4$ in.

SMALL ROLLING CUPBOARD

Sides
- Two pieces
  $25^1/_{32}$ x $20^7/_8$ x $5/_8$ in.

Fascia
- One piece
  28 x $25^{13}/_{32}$ x $3/_8$ in.

Base
- One piece
  $25^7/_8$ x $21^7/_{16}$ x $5/_8$ in.

Top
- One piece
  $21^7/_{16}$ x $2^3/_4$ x $5/_8$ in.

Back
- One piece
  $21^7/_{16}$ x $5^3/_4$ x $5/_8$ in.

Front
- One piece
  $21^7/_{16}$ x 7 x $5/_8$ in.

LARGE ROLLING CUPBOARD

Sides
- Two pieces
  $47^{13}/_{32}$ x $14^3/_{16}$ x $5/_8$ in.

Fascia
- One piece
  52 x $15^5/_8$ x $3/_8$ in.

Back
- One piece
  $37^1/_8$ x $21^7/_{16}$ x $3/_8$ in.

Top
- One piece
  $21^7/_{16}$ x $18^{15}/_{16}$ x $5/_8$ in.

Base
- One piece
  $21^7/_{16}$ x $14^3/_{16}$ x $3/_4$ in.

Shelf
- Two pieces
  $20^3/_{16}$ x $14^3/_{16}$ x $3/_4$ in.

BROOM CUPBOARD

Sides
- Two pieces
  $60^7/_{16}$ x $9^{27}/_{32}$ x $5/_8$ in.

Back
- One piece
  $53^{23}/_{32}$ x $21^7/_8$ x $3/_8$ in.
- One piece
  $52^3/_4$ x 4 x $3/_8$ in.

Top
- One piece
  $21^7/_8$ x $13^9/_{16}$ x $5/_8$ in.

Base
- One piece
  $21^7/_8$ x $9^{27}/_{32}$ x $3/_4$ in.

Door
- One piece
  $61^7/_8$ x $3^3/_4$ x $5/_8$ in.
- One piece
  $61^1/_4$ x $18^5/_{32}$ x $5/_8$ in.

PARTITIONS
- One piece
  $39^{31}/_{32}$ x $21^7/_{16}$ x $3/_4$ in.
- One piece
  $26^{11}/_{16}$ x $21^7/_{16}$ x $3/_4$ in.

- Diagrams and templates on pages 116–117
- Jigsaw
- Drill
- $3/_{16}$ in. and $1/_8$ in. drill bits
- Countersink bit
- Tape measure
- Pencil
- Wood glue
- Screwdriver

Screws
- 85: $1^3/_8$ in.
- 60: 1 in.
- 22: $3/_4$ in.
- 60: $1/_2$ in.

- Twelve fixed castors with $1^7/_8$ in. diameter wheels and measuring $2^5/_8$ in. from the bottom of the wheel to the fixing plate.
- Plane
- Eight right-angled metal plates with suitable screws
- Filling knife
- Filler
- Sanding block
- 120-grit sandpaper
- Paintbrush
- Primer
- Satin paint
- Four handles

Medium Rolling Cupboard

1 Enlarge the side template by 1,000 percent and transfer it onto the two side pieces (see Template Techniques, page 112). Using a jigsaw, cut out the shapes (see Cutting with a Jigsaw, page 17). Predrill and countersink the marked ³⁄₁₆ in. holes (see Drilling and Countersinking, page 12). Enlarge the fascia template by 1,000 percent and transfer it onto the fascia piece. Using a jigsaw, cut out the shape.

2 Predrill and countersink the following ³⁄₁₆ in. holes.
In the back panel, drill four holes on both long sides and one short (bottom) side, ¼ in. in from the edge. Position one hole 3 in. from each end, with two holes spaced evenly between them. Draw a line 16½ in. from the bottom side and position one hole 2½ in. from each end, with one more hole centrally between them.
In the top piece, drill three holes on both short sides, ¼ in. in from the edge. Position one hole 2¾ in. from each end, one more hole centrally between them.
In the base piece, drill three holes on both short sides, ¼ in. in from the edge. Position one hole 2 in from each end, one more hole centrally between them.

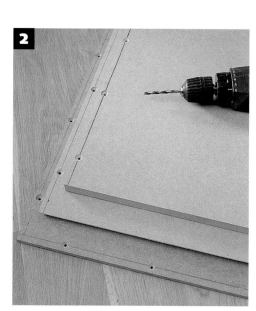

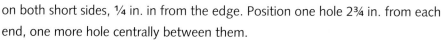

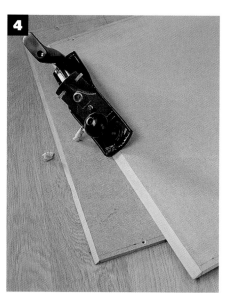

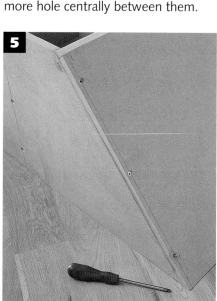

3 Butt the short, square edge of one side piece against a short side of the base. Drill pilot holes through the predrilled holes in the base into the edge of the side piece. Glue and screw the two pieces together, driving 1³⁄₈ in. screws into the pilot holes (see Joining Two Pieces with Screws, page 13). Attach the other side piece to the other end of the base piece in the same way.

4 On the top piece draw a line ½ in. from one long edge. Using a plane, chamfer the edge up to the drawn line. Turn the top over and mark another line ³⁄₈ in. from the other long edge. Chamfer this edge in the same way. On the back piece draw a line ¼ in. from the short edge that is not drilled. Chamfer this edge in the same way as the top piece.

5 Lay the top piece against the sloping ends of the side pieces, with one chamfered edge aligned with the points and the other flush with the straight edges, as shown. Drill pilot holes and glue and screw the two pieces together, driving 1³⁄₈ in. screws through the predrilled holes in the top piece into the pilot holes.

6 Lay the back piece over the frame, with the chamfered edge at the top and all edges aligned. Drill pilot holes and glue and screw the pieces together, driving 1 in. screws through the predrilled holes in the back piece into the pilot holes. Predrill, countersink, and then pilot drill three evenly spaced holes in the chamfered edge of the back piece into the chamfered edge of the top piece. Drive 1 in. screws through the predrilled holes into the pilot holes.

7 Slide the shelf into the cupboard, aligning it with the predrilled holes in the side pieces. Drill pilot holes and glue and screw the shelf in position, driving 1⅜ in. screws through the predrilled holes in the side pieces into the pilot holes.

8 Position one castor 2 in. from each corner of the base. Drill pilot holes through the holes in the castor plate and screw the castor in position, driving ½ in. screws into the pilot holes.

9 Predrill and countersink six 3/16 in. holes in the fascia piece, 1¼ in. in from the edge, spacing three holes evenly along the long side, two holes on the short side, and one   hole centrally on the sloping top side. Lay the cupboard on the side that will be the back. Lay the fascia piece over the front of the cupboard, positioning it so that it sits 1½ in. above the bottoms of the castors and centrally side-to-side. Drill pilot holes through the predrilled holes into the front of the cupboard. Glue and screw the pieces together, driving ¾ in. screws through the predrilled holes into the pilot holes.

Simply slide the cupboards into their slots to instantly declutter your hallway.

Small Rolling Cupboard

1 Enlarge the side template by 1,000 percent and transfer it onto the two side pieces. Using a jigsaw, cut out the shapes. Enlarge the fascia template by 1,000 percent and transfer it onto the fascia piece. Using a jigsaw, cut out the shape.

2 Predrill and countersink the following ³⁄₁₆ in. holes.

In the base piece, drill five holes on both long sides, ¼ in. in from the edge. Position one hole 2 in. from one end, and another hole 2¾ in. from the opposite end, with three more holes spaced evenly between them.

In the top piece, drill one hole on both short sides, ¼ in. in from the edge. Position the holes ½ in. from one long edge.

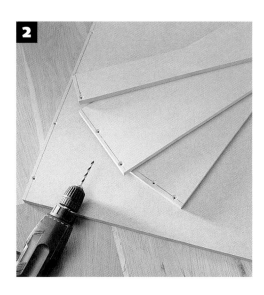

In the back piece, drill two holes on both short sides, ¼ in. in from the edge. Position one hole 1¾ in. and another 3 in. from one long edge.

In the front piece, drill two holes on both short sides, ¼ in. in from the edge. Position one hole 1¾ in. and another 4¼ in. from one long edge.

3 On the base, top, and back pieces draw a line ½ in. from one long edge. Using a plane, chamfer the edge up to the drawn line following Step 4 of Medium Rolling Cupboard (see page 32). Butt the long, straight edge of one side piece against a long square side of the base. Drill pilot holes through the predrilled holes in the base into the edge of the side piece. Glue and screw the pieces together, driving 1⅜ in. screws into the pilot holes. Attach the other side piece to the other end of the base in the same way.

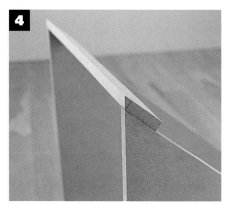

4 Lay the top piece across the tops of the side pieces, with the chamfered edge flush with the points, as shown. Drill pilot holes through the predrilled holes in the top piece into the edges of the side pieces. Glue and screw the pieces together, driving 1⅜ in. screws through the predrilled holes into the pilot holes.

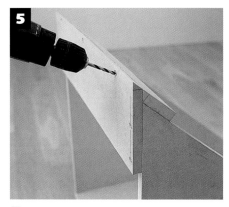

5 Lay the back piece across the backs of the side pieces, with the chamfered edge flush with the upper edge of the top piece, as shown. Drill pilot holes through the predrilled holes in the back piece into the edges of the side pieces. Glue and screw the pieces together, driving 1⅜ in. screws through the predrilled holes into the pilot holes. Predrill, countersink, and then pilot drill three evenly spaced holes in the chamfered edge of the back piece into the chamfered edge of the top piece. Drive 1 in. screws through the predrilled holes into the pilot holes.

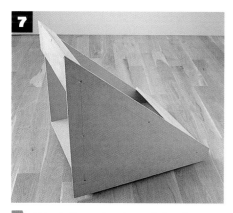

6 Lay the front piece across the lower ends of the side pieces, with the chamfered edge flush with the points as shown. Drill pilot holes through the predrilled holes in the front piece into the edges of the side pieces. Glue and screw the pieces together, driving 1⅜ in. screws through the predrilled holes into the pilot holes.

7 Attach the wheels and the fascia piece to the cupboard following steps 8–9 of Medium Rolling Cupboard (see page 33)

Large Rolling Cupboard

Make up the large rolling cupboard following the instructions for the Medium Rolling Cupboard (see page 32). This large cupboard has two shelves; six holes must be drilled in each long side of the back and eight evenly spaced screws used to attach the fascia piece.

Broom Cupboard

Make up the body of the broom cupboard following Steps 1–6 of *Medium Rolling Cupboard* (see page 32). Drill eight holes in each long side of the back.

1 On the door strip predrill and countersink seven holes on the right-hand long side, ¼ in. in from the edge. Position one hole 2 in. from each end, with five more holes spaced evenly between them. On the short (bottom) sides, position one hole 1½ in. and another hole 3⅛ in. from the drilled side, ¼ in. in from the edge. Rabbet two butt hinges across the door strip and the door, positioning the hinges 5 in. from the top and bottom (see Steps 1–3 of Rabbeting a Butt Hinge, page 19).

2 Lay the door strip along the edge of the cupboard you want the door to hinge on. Drill pilot holes through the predrilled holes in the door strip into the edge of the cupboard side. Glue and screw the pieces together, driving 1⅜ in. screws through the predrilled holes into the pilot holes. Screw the hinges to the rabbets in the door strip. Lay the door in place and screw the other side of the hinges to it.

Fitting the Cupboards and Partitions

Screw the narrow partition piece to the back of the broom cupboard, ⅜ in. in from the outer edge. Fit the broom cupboard in under the stairs and screw it in place. Use suitable wall fixings to attach it to the wall and screws to attach it to the underside of the stairs. Stand the other two partitions in place, spacing them to accommodate the rolling cupboards. Use angled metal plates and suitable screws to attach the partitions to the floor and the underside of the stairs. Fill all screw holes, sand the elements of the cupboard, and prime them, then paint them with two coats of satin paint (see Finishing Techniques, page 110). Fit a handle to the front of each rolling cupboard and one to the broom cupboard door.

Hallway Seat

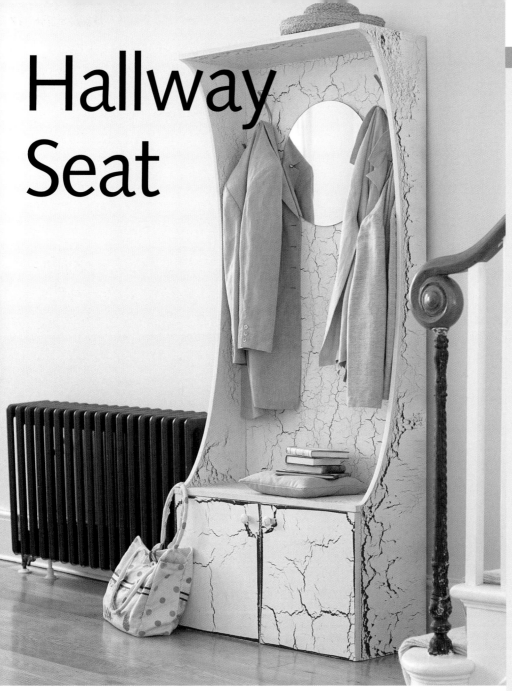

YOU WILL NEED

MDF

Sides
- Two pieces 71½ x 12 x ¾ in.

Top and base
- Two pieces 32 x 12 x ¾ in.

Back
- One piece 73 x 32 x ½ in.

Seat
- One piece 32 x 12¾ x ¾ in.

Feet
- Four pieces 1 x 1 x ⅜ in.

Doors
- Two pieces 17 x 15¹⁵⁄₁₆ x ¾ in.

- Template on page 115
- Jigsaw
- Drill
- ³⁄₁₆ in. and ⅛ in. drill bits
- Countersink bit
- Tape measure
- Pencil
- Wood glue
- Screwdriver

Screws
- 41: 1⅜ in.
- 8: 1½ in.
- 4: 1 in.
- 32: ½ in.
- 2: ½ in. mirror screws with decorative caps

- Four lay-on hinges
- Filling knife
- Filler
- Sanding block
- 120-grit sandpaper
- Paintbrush
- Primer
- Satin paint
- Two door handles
- Four coat hooks
- Mirror with two drilled holes

The primary requirements for a piece of hallway furniture are that it be slim and multifunctional. Most hallways are too small to accommodate bulky furniture or anything that does not provide adequate storage. This seat not only provides somewhere to sit, it also offers space for hanging coats, a shelf for hats, a cupboard for shoes, and a mirror.

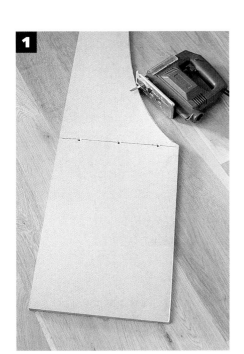

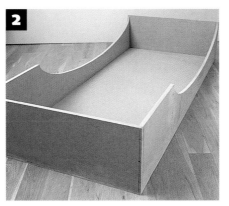

1 Enlarge the template by 667 percent and transfer it onto the side pieces (see Template Techniques, page 112). Using a jigsaw, cut out the shapes (see Cutting with a Jigsaw, page 17). Predrill and countersink the marked ³⁄₁₆ in. holes (see Drilling and Countersinking, page 12).

Also predrill and countersink the following ³⁄₁₆ in. holes.

In the top and base pieces, predrill and countersink ³⁄₁₆ in. holes on the short sides, ³⁄₈ in. in from the edge. Position one hole 2 in. from each end, with one more hole centrally between them.

In the back piece, drill holes along each side, ³⁄₈ in. in from the edge. Position one hole 2¼ in. from each corner. On the short sides, space three holes evenly between them, and on the long sides, seven holes. Measure up and draw a line 16⅝ in. from one short (bottom) end. Predrill and countersink five holes on this line. Position one hole 2¼ in. from each edge, with three more holes spaced evenly between them.

2 Using the side, top, base, and back pieces and 1⅜ in. screws, make up the body of the seat, following steps 1–5 of Basic Cupboard (see page 20).

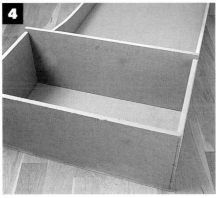

3 On the seat piece, draw a pencil line ¾ in. in from each short edge. Draw another line ¾ in. from one long side. Using a jigsaw, cut out long notches on the short sides following the pencil lines.

4 Slide the seat piece into the body of the hallway seat, aligning the edges with the rows of holes in the sides and back. Using a ⅛ in. drill bit, drill pilot holes through the predrilled holes in the sides and back into the edges of the seat piece. Glue and screw the pieces together, driving 1½ in. screws through the predrilled holes into the pilot holes. Attach the feet following Step 8 of Basic Blanket Box (see page 18).

5 Hang the doors using lay-on hinges and ½ in. screws (see Hanging a Door Using Lay-On Hinges, page 23). Fill all screw holes, sand the whole hallway seat, and prime it, then paint it with two coats of satin paint (see Finishing Techniques, page 110 or Customizing the Seat, below). Attach the door handles. Attach the coat hooks to the seat back, using the fittings supplied with them, and the mirror, using ½ in. screws with decorative caps.

Customizing
THE SEAT

Bold paint finishes work well on furniture with simple lines. This seat was painted deep crimson and then crackle-glazed in light cream. The effect is striking, but as the overall color is pale, it is not overpowering in a small space.

The Living Room

This room often has to be all things to all people and, as such, needs to be well organized and look good. Creating storage that satisfies both agendas is not as hard as you might think.

Telephone Table

Elegant yet practical, this table will suit a modern or traditionally styled home. The slatted shelf will hold directories and the drawer will hide away the pens and notepads that usually clutter up the space around the telephone. This project is made from solid wood; beech was used here, but any close-grained wood will be suitable.

YOU WILL NEED

Sides

Beech

- Four pieces 9 x 1⅛ x ¾ in.
- Eight pieces 24 x 1⅛ x ¾ in.

Shelf

Beech

- Two pieces 8¾ x ¾ x ¾ in.
- Four pieces 12½ x 1⅛ x ¾ in.

Drawer case

Beech

- One piece 12½ x 3¾ x ¾ in.
- Two pieces 7¼ x 3¾ x ¾ in.

MDF

- One piece 12¼ x 7⅞ x ¼ in.

Top

Beech

- Two pieces 15½ x 5¼ x ¾ in.

Drawer

Beech

- One piece 12⁷⁄₁₆ x 4¼ x ⅝ in.

MDF

- Two pieces 10⅞ x 3⅜ x ⅜ in.
- Two pieces 6⅜ x 3⅜ x ½ in.
- One piece 10⅞ x 7⅛ x ¼ in.

- Tape measure
- Pencil
- Jigsaw
- Drill
- ³⁄₁₆ in. and ⅛ in. drill bits
- Countersink bit
- Wood glue
- Screwdriver
- Short screwdriver

Screws

- 24: 1½ in.
- 16: 1 in.
- 4: 1⅜ in.
- 10: ¾ in.

- Staple gun
- ⅝ in. staples
- 120-grit sandpaper
- Tung oil

1 Butt two of the short side pieces together, narrow faces up. Draw lines across both pieces at ⁹⁄₁₆ in. and 3³⁄₁₆ in. from each end. Predrill a ³⁄₁₆ in. hole on each line, positioning the holes in the middle of the lines. Turn the pieces over and countersink these holes (see Drilling and Countersinking, page 12). Turn the pieces back over and draw additional lines across both pieces at 1⅛ in., 2⅝ in., and 3¾ in. from each end. Choose one piece to be the top piece and on this piece only draw lines, predrill, and countersink holes at 1½ in. and 4⅛ in. from each end.

2 Butt one end of one long side piece against one end of the bottom piece, aligning the inner edge of the long piece with the pencil

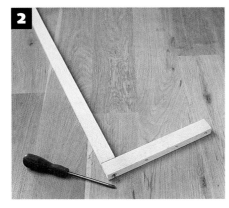

mark on the bottom piece. Using a ⅛ in. drill bit, drill a pilot hole through the predrilled hole in the bottom piece into the end of the long piece. Glue and screw the two pieces together, driving 1½ in. screws through the predrilled holes into the pilot holes (see Joining Two Pieces with Screws, page 13). Attach the top piece to the other end of the long piece in the same way.

3 Fix three more long pieces between the bottom and top pieces in the same way, aligning the ends of the long pieces with the pencil marks on the top and

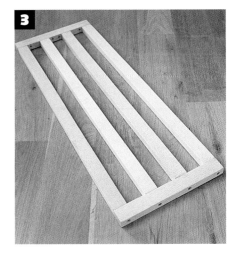

bottom pieces and using 1½ in. screws. Follow Steps 1–3 with the remaining side pieces to make up the other side of the table.

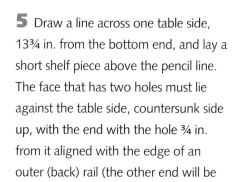

4 Butt the two short shelf pieces together and draw lines across one face of both pieces, ⅜ in. and 3³⁄₁₆ in. from each end. Predrill and countersink a ³⁄₁₆ in. hole on each line, positioning the holes in the middle of the lines. Turn the pieces on their sides and draw lines across both of them, 1¹⁄₁₆ in. and 5⅞ in. from one end. Countersink these holes on opposite sides of the pieces, so that they mirror one another.

5 Draw a line across one table side, 13¾ in. from the bottom end, and lay a short shelf piece above the pencil line. The face that has two holes must lie against the table side, countersunk side up, with the end with the hole ¾ in. from it aligned with the edge of an outer (back) rail (the other end will be short of the front rail). The four holes drilled in the other face must have the countersunk side facing the bottom of the table side. Using a ⅛ in. drill bit, drill pilot holes through the predrilled holes in the shelf piece into the two aligning rails of the table side. Screw (but do not glue) the pieces together, driving 1 in. screws through the predrilled holes into the pilot holes.

6 On the short shelf piece, mark exactly where the rails of the table side cross it. Make the marks on the face that has not been countersunk. Unscrew the piece and extend the pencil lines onto the face that was against the table side. Repeat Steps 5–6 with the other table side and short shelf piece.

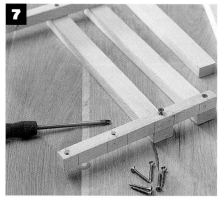

7 Lay one long shelf piece between the two short pieces, aligning it with a set of the pencil marks made in Step 6. Drill pilot holes through the predrilled holes in each short piece into the long piece. Glue and screw the long piece to the short pieces, driving 1 in. screws through the predrilled holes into the pilot holes. Attach the remaining long pieces between the short pieces in the same way.

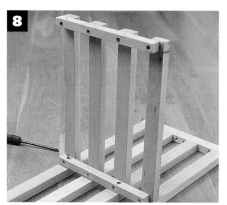

8 Glue and screw one short shelf piece back onto a table side piece in the same way as in Step 5. Attach the other table side to the other end of the shelf in the same way.

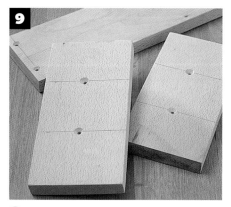

9 Predrill and countersink the beech drawer case pieces. On the short pieces, position one hole 2⅜ in. from each end and centrally across the width. On the long piece, position two holes on each short side, ½ in. from the edge and ¾ in. from each end.

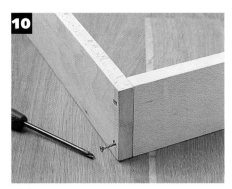

10 Butt the edge of one short (side) drawer tray piece against one end of the long (back) drawer tray piece. The countersunk holes in the side piece must face inward. Drill pilot holes through the predrilled holes in the back piece into the edge of the side piece. Glue and screw the pieces together, driving 1⅜ in. screws through the predrilled holes into the pilot holes. Attach the other side piece to the other end of the back piece in the same way.

11 Lay the MDF (base) drawer tray piece over the edges of the sides and back, positioning it centrally. Glue and staple it in place, firing staples through the base into the edges of the sides and back (see Joining Two Pieces with Staples, page 28).

12 Slide the drawer tray between the table sides, aligning the top of the tray with the tops of the sides and the back of the tray with the backs of the sides. Drill pilot holes through the predrilled holes in the tray sides into the aligning rails in the table sides. Glue and screw the pieces together, driving 1 in. screws through the predrilled holes into the pilot holes.

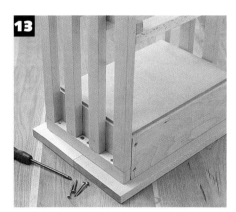

13 Butt the long edges of the top pieces together and lay them facedown. Stand the rest of the table upside down on top of them, positioning it centrally. Drill pilot holes through the predrilled holes in the table sides into the top pieces. Glue and screw the pieces together, driving 1½ in. screws through the predrilled holes into the pilot holes.

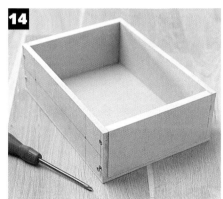

14 In one long MDF drawer piece, predrill and countersink two ³⁄₁₆ in. holes, positioning them 1½ in. from each end and centrally across the width. Using the five MDF drawer pieces and ¾ in. screws, make up a drawer using the blanket box principle (see Basic Blanket Box, page 16). The countersunk side of the holes, in the center of one long side, face inward.

15 Lay the beech drawer piece facedown and stand the drilled side of the MDF drawer on top of it. Align the top of the drawer with one long edge of the beech piece and position it centrally side-to-side. Drill pilot holes through the predrilled holes in the drawer into the beech. Glue and screw the pieces together, driving ¾ in. screws through the predrilled holes into the pilot holes. Slide the drawer into the tray. Carefully sand off any pencil marks and oil the beech to protect it and to bring out the color of the wood.

Floating Shelf

This contemporary curved shelf

is designed to display

knickknacks and plants, rather

than to hold heavy books.

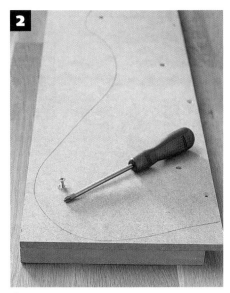

1 Enlarge the template by 400 percent and transfer it onto the thin piece of MDF (see Template Techniques, page 112). Predrill and countersink the marked ³⁄₁₆ in. holes (see Drilling and Countersinking, page 12).

2 Glue and screw the thin piece of MDF to the thick piece, aligning the front edge of the thin piece with one long edge of the thick piece (see Joining Two Pieces with Screws, page 13). Drive 1 in. screws through the five holes **not** marked with a star on the template.

3 Using a jigsaw, cut out the shape (see Cutting with a Jigsaw, page 17).

4 Drill three ³⁄₁₆ in. holes in the piece of lumber. Position the holes centrally on one face, with one hole 6 in. from each end and one centrally between them.

5 Fit the piece of lumber into the rabbet at the back of the shelf. Sand the ends of the lumber flush with the edges of the shelf, then remove the lumber. Fill the screw holes with screws in them, sand the whole shelf and the lumber, and prime, then paint with two coats of satin paint (see Finishing Techniques, page 110).

TO HANG THE SHELF

Drill three holes in a straight line in the wall, spaced to match the three holes in the lumber. Fit wall fixings suitable for the wall into the holes (see Hanging Items on Walls, page 113). Position the lumber in front of the holes and drive appropriate screws through the predrilled holes in the lumber into the wall. Fit the shelf over the lumber and drive 1¼ in. screws down through the remaining four predrilled holes. Fill these screw holes, sand them, and touch up the paint.

Television Cabinet

Wide-screen televisions are wonderful to watch, but they are not decorative and they can dominate a room. This country-style cabinet holds a 32 in. television, plus its peripherals. The tongue-and-groove doors hide everything away when it is not in use and present an attractive face to the world.

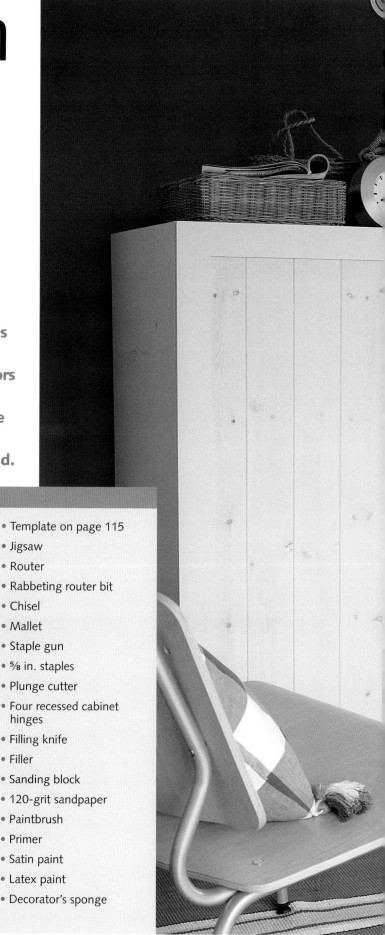

YOU WILL NEED

Sides

MDF

- Two pieces
  38¾ x 28½ x ⅝ in.

Top and base

MDF

- Two pieces
  41 x 28½ x ⅝ in.

Shelf

MDF

- One piece
  38¾ x 28¾ x ¾ in.

Back

MDF

- One piece 41 x 40 x ⅜ in.

Doors

MDF

- Two pieces
  20⁷⁄₁₆ x 40 x ⅝ in.

Tongue-and-groove

- Enough ½ in. thick,
  35½ in. long planks to fill
  two 16 in. wide holes

Feet

Lumber

- Four pieces
  4 x 2¾ x 1½ in.

- Tape measure
- Pencil
- Drill
- ³⁄₁₆ in., ⅛ in., and ½ in
  drill bits
- Countersink bit
- Wood glue
- Screwdriver

Screws

- 38: 1⅜ in.
- 30: 1¼ in.
- 16: ¼ in.

- Template on page 115
- Jigsaw
- Router
- Rabbeting router bit
- Chisel
- Mallet
- Staple gun
- ⅝ in. staples
- Plunge cutter
- Four recessed cabinet
  hinges
- Filling knife
- Filler
- Sanding block
- 120-grit sandpaper
- Paintbrush
- Primer
- Satin paint
- Latex paint
- Decorator's sponge

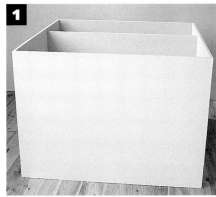

1 Using the side, top, base, shelf, and back pieces, make up the body of the cabinet, following steps 1–6 of Basic Cupboard (see page 20). Position the shelf 14 in. up from the base and drill five holes through each side piece and six through the back piece to attach it. Drill six holes along each edge of the back piece and use 1¼ in. screws to attach the back to the cabinet. Fill all screw holes, sand the cabinet, and prime it, then paint it with two coats of satin paint (see Finishing Techniques, page 110).

2 Enlarge the template by 200 percent and transfer it onto the feet pieces (see Template Techniques, page 112). Using a jigsaw, cut out the shapes (see Cutting with a Jigsaw, page 17). Sand, prime, and paint the feet. Position one foot on each corner of the cabinet base, 2 in. in from the corner. Using a ⅛ in. drill bit, drill and countersink two pilot holes through the base into the top of each foot. Glue and screw the pieces together, using 1⅜ in. screws.

3 Draw a line 2½ in. in from each edge of both door pieces. Cut out, rabbet and chisel the door frames (see Making a Door Frame, page 49).

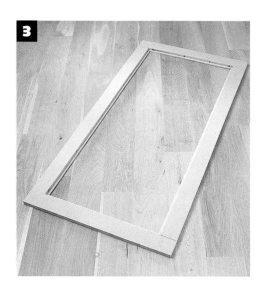

4 Select enough tongue-and-groove planks to fill one door frame. Using a jigsaw, cut the tongue off one plank and the groove off another. These planks are the outer ones of the panel.

customizing
THE CABINET

Before making the cabinet, check the dimensions of your television, and if necessary, alter the dimensions of the cabinet, and quantity of MDF, to suit. You can change the whole look of the cabinet by the way in which you treat the doors. For a more contemporary look, fit aluminum panels into the rabbets (see Dry Goods Cupboard, page 56), or make solid doors and paint them. For a softer effect you could staple fabric into the rabbets; consider using a fabric that matches soft furnishings in the room for a very coordinated look.

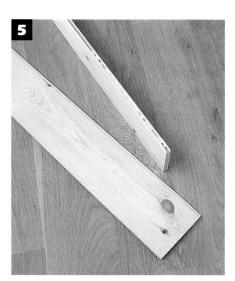

5 Run a line of wood glue along the groove in one plank. Push the tongue of another plank firmly into the glued groove, aligning the tops and bottoms. Wipe away any excess adhesive with a damp cloth. Repeat the process until you have made up a panel wide enough to fill a door frame. Remember that the tongueless and grooveless planks go on the outside edges of the panel. Make up another panel for the other door frame in the same way.

6 Lay a tongue-and-groove panel in the rabbet on the back of a door frame. Glue and staple it in place, firing staples through the tongue-and-groove into the frame (see Joining Two Pieces with Staples, page 28). Sand, prime, and paint the door frames. Dilute some latex (emulsion) paint— the same color as the satin— with water, mixing one part water to one part paint. Use this mixture to paint the tongue-and-groove panels. Let the paint settle a little and then wipe it back with a sponge. This allows the grain of the wood to show through. Once dry, seal the panel with satin-finish varnish.

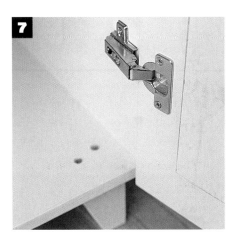

7 Hang the doors, one on either side of the cabinet, using recessed hinges (see Hanging a Door Using Recessed Hinges, page 59).

MAKING A DOOR FRAME

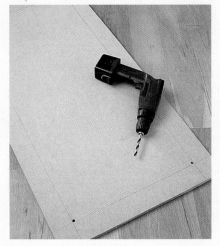

1 Draw a line the same distance in from each edge of the door piece. The measured distance will be the width of the door frame. Using a ½ in. drill bit, drill a hole in each corner of the inner rectangle, just inside the drawn lines.

2 Slip the blade of a jigsaw into one of the drilled holes and cut carefully along the drawn line until you reach the next hole. Turn the blade and cut along the next line. Continue the process until you have cut out the whole panel. Carefully sand out any small irregularities in the corners.

3 Fit a rabbeting bit into a router. Place the router on the edge of the back of the door frame and rout a rabbet right around it.

4 To square off the rounded corners, place a chisel against the drawn line in the corner, with the angled face of the chisel pointing into the rabbet. Chisel down to the depth of the rabbet. Chisel around the whole corner. The MDF fragments will usually just fall away, but you can use the tip of the chisel to pry them free if necessary.

DVD and CD Rack

This is a clever, flexible design for a rack that can be made in different sizes to hold large or small collections of music and films. The rack can be hung vertically or horizontally and takes up little space while providing plenty of efficient storage.

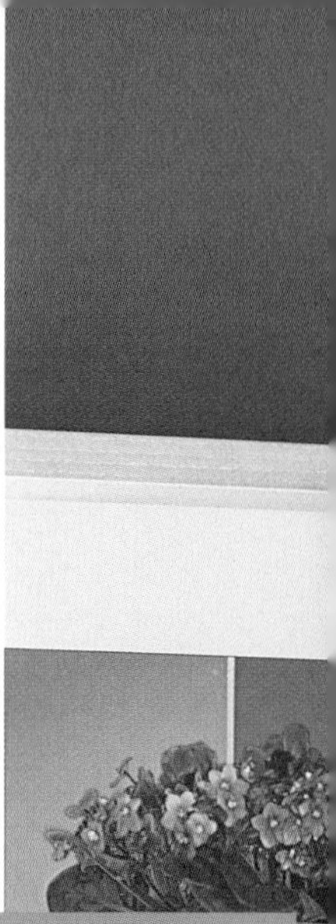

1 Assemble one section, as shown in the tinted section of the diagram on page 118. Start by drawing a pencil line 5½ in. from the left-hand side of one longer large compartment divider.

Diagram on page 118

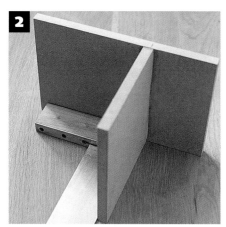

2 Stand one small compartment divider to the left of the line, butting the edge right up to the line. Glue and staple the pieces together, firing staples through the long divider into the edge of the small one (see Joining Two Pieces with Staples, page 28). Use a try square to ensure that the pieces are at right angles (see Using a Try Square, page 13). Repeat with one shorter large compartment divider and one small compartment divider.

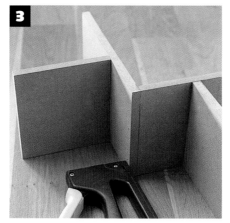

3 Place the longer divider on a worksurface, standing it on its long edge, and with the small divider pointing to the left. Lay the shorter divider on a long side, with the small divider pointing to the right. Butt the short edge of the shorter divider against the end of the longer divider. Glue and staple the dividers together, firing staples through the longer divider into the edge of the shorter one.

YOU WILL NEED

MDF

Large compartment dividers
- Three pieces 9⅜ x 5¾ x ½ in.
- Three pieces 8⅞ x 5¾ x ½ in.

Small compartment dividers
- Six pieces 5½ x 5¾ x ½ in.

Sides
- Two pieces 46⅝ x 5¾ x ½ in.

Back
- One piece 46⅝ x 15⅞ x ¼ in.

Horizontal dividers
- Four pieces 14⅞ x 5¾ x ½ in.

- Diagram on page 118
- Tape measure
- Pencil
- Wood glue
- Staple gun
- ⅝ in. staples
- Try square
- Drill
- ³⁄₁₆ in. and ⅛ in. drill bits
- Screwdriver

Screws
- 16: 1 in.
- 4: suitable for wall fixings

- Filling knife and filler
- Sanding block
- 120-grit sandpaper
- Paintbrush
- Primer
- Satin paint
- Suitable wall fixings

4 The result of Steps 1–3 should make a unit that looks like this (ignore the g-clamp, it's just there for support). Repeat the steps with the remaining compartment dividers to produce three identical shapes.

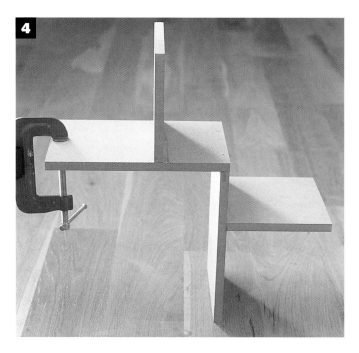

5 Predrill and countersink eight holes in both of the side pieces (see Drilling and Countersinking, page 12). Position two holes ¼ in. in from each short end and 1½ in. in from the corners. Position two more holes 11¾ in. from each short end and 1½ in. in from the sides.

6 Position one of the horizontal dividers lengthwise between the ends of the side pieces. Using a ⅛ in. drill bit, drill pilot holes through the predrilled holes in the side pieces into the edges of the divider. Glue and screw the pieces together, driving screws through the predrilled holes into the pilot holes (see Joining Two Pieces with Screws, page 13).

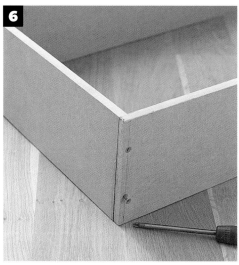

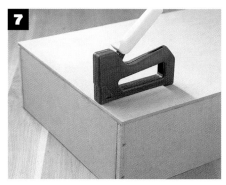

7 Lay the back over these pieces and glue and staple it to them, firing staples through the back into the edges. The result is a box that is open at one end.

8 Turn the box over. Run a line of glue down each edge on one face of a unit. Lay the unit in thc box, following the diagram on page 118. Glue and staple the ends of the compartment dividers to the sides and end of the box, firing staples through the box into the ends of the dividers.

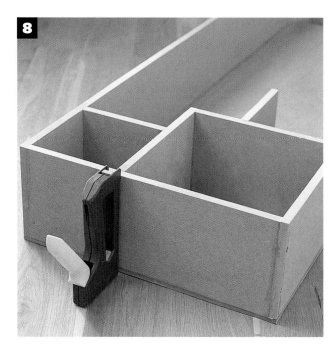

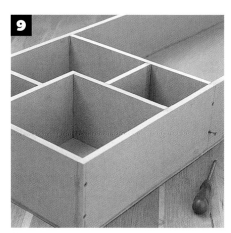

9 Position a second horizontal divider, making sure that it is square in the box and aligned with the predrilled holes in the sides. Glue and screw the divider in place, as in Step 6.

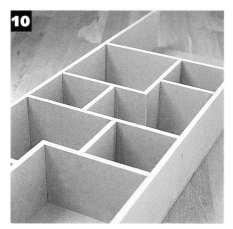

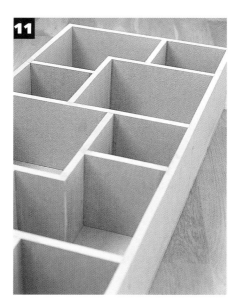

10 Repeat the process, turning the next unit the other way around, as shown in the diagram.

11 Fasten the final unit in the box, making sure that it is round in the same way as the first one. Glue and screw the final divider in place at the end of the box. Fill all screw holes, sand the whole rack, and prime it, then paint it with two coats of satin paint (see Finishing Techniques, page 110). Drill a hole in each corner of the back and use suitable fixings for your wall to hang the rack (see Hanging Items on Walls, page 113).

customizing THE RACK

The sections in the rack are the same size whether it is hung vertically or horizontally, and it provides good storage for books and ornaments, as well as CDs and DVDs. You can alter the size of the rack by adding more or fewer of the separate units, just remember to alter the length of the sides to suit. If you are making a longer rack than this one, then you should use additional wall fixings in the middle of the length when you hang it.

The
Kitchen

Whether you prefer a built-in kitchen or the increasingly popular "unfitted" style, well-considered, efficient storage is a must in this room. Here are practical yet stylish projects for traditional and modern kitchens alike.

YOU WILL NEED

Top and base

MDF

- Two pieces 24 x 4 x ⅝ in.

Sides

MDF

- Two pieces
  76¾ x 4 x ⅝ in.

Plinth

MDF

- One piece
  22¾ x 5½ x ⅝ in.

Shelves

MDF

- Ten pieces
  22¾ x 4 x ⅝ in.

Back

MDF

- One piece
  78 x 24 x ¼ in.

Doors

MDF

- Two pieces
  36¼ x 24⅞ x ⅝ in.

Aluminum sheet

- Two pieces
  32¼ x 20⅞ in.

- Tape measure

- Pencil

- Drill

- ³⁄₁₆ in., ⅛ in., and ½ in.
  drill bits

- Countersink bit

- Wood glue

- Screwdriver

Screws

- 54: 1⅜ in.

- 24: 1 in.

- 16: ½ in.

- Jigsaw

- Router

- Rabbeting router bit

- 120-grit sandpaper

- Sanding block

- Instant grab gap-filling
  adhesive

- Plunge cutter

- Four recessed
  cabinet hinges

- Filling knife

- Filler

- Primer

- Satin paint

- Paintbrush

- Two door handles

Dry Goods Cupboard

Deep cupboards are a problem when it comes to storing dry goods. Things get pushed to the back and can't be found, so you buy another, only to find the original item when you are looking for something else. This slim cupboard has two advantages over traditional deep kitchen cupboards; it's shallow, so you can see exactly what you've got, and it takes up very little room, so it's suitable for the smallest kitchen, or even a corridor. The height of the cupboard and the number of shelves mean that even just one of these cupboards will hold a surprising amount.

1 Using the top, base, sides, plinth, shelf, and back pieces, and 1⅜ in. and 1 in. screws, make up the body of the cupboard following the instructions for Basic Bookcase (see page 10). However, as the MDF used for this cupboard is ⅝ in. thick, as opposed to the ¾ in. MDF used for the bookcase, all predrilling must be done ¼ in. in from the edges and up from marked shelf lines. For advice on spacing the shelves, turn to Customizing the Cupboard, (see page 58).

2 Draw a pencil line 4 in. in from each edge of the door pieces to establish rectangular panels within the doors. Using a ½ in. drill bit and a jigsaw, cut out the panels and rabbet the frame (see Steps 1–3 of Making a Door Frame, page 49).

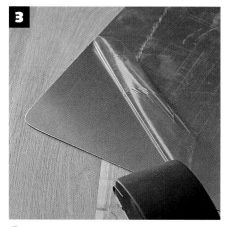

3 Round the corners of the pieces of aluminum with sandpaper, so that they fit into the rabbets on the back of the doors.

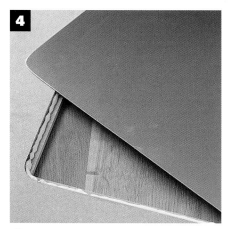

4 Run a line of adhesive around the rabbet in the back of each door. Press a piece of aluminum in on top of it and wipe away any excess adhesive. Leave to dry.

customizing
THE CUPBOARD

Dry goods are commonly packaged in a range of standard sizes, so take time to consider the types of goods you want to store and space the shelves to suit. There will, of course, be exceptions to this standard packaging, so either allow a little extra space on each shelf or make one shelf much more spacious to accommodate a variety of goods. Always space the shelves so that one shelf is in the middle of the cupboard, where the doors meet. The panels in the doors can be made from a number of materials, so choose something to suit the style of your kitchen. Aluminum or glass is very appropriate for a modern kitchen; chicken wire or thin wood would suit a more traditional style. Here handles incorporating name plates have been used to make finding the right item even easier.

5 Hang the doors using recessed hinges and ½ in. screws (see Hanging a Door Using Recessed Hinges, page 59). The bottom edge of the lower door should overlap the lowest shelf in the cupboard and the top edge should lie against the edge of a shelf. Fill all screw holes, sand the cupboard, and prime it, then paint it with two coats of satin paint (see Finishing Techniques, page 110). Attach a handle to each door.

HANGING A DOOR USING RECESSED HINGES

1 Draw a horizontal line on the back of the door where you want a hinge to lie; approximately 8 in. from the top and bottom, depending on any shelves within the body of the furniture. Fold the hinge closed and position the recessed section of the hinge centrally on the line. Lay a scrap piece of wood—the same thickness as the sides of the body— against the upright, closed part of the hinge. Position the hinge and wood so that the outer edge of the scrap piece is flush with the edge of the door. Mark the position of the recessed section.

2 Using a drill and plunge cutter, cut a hole at the marked points. Cut to the depth of the recessed section, being especially careful not to cut all the way through the door. Put the recessed section of the hinge into the hole and make a pencil mark through the screw hole on each side. Remove the hinge and drill a pilot hole at each marked point.

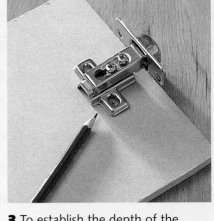

3 To establish the depth of the hinge on the inside of the cupboard, start by setting the adjustment screw on the hinge to the central position. Lay the closed hinge on a scrap piece of wood, with the plate of the recessed section butted up to the edge. Make a pencil mark through each screw hole. Measure the distance from the edge of the MDF to the pencil marks.

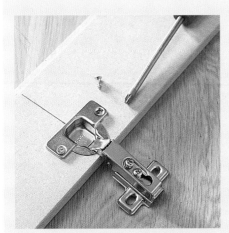

4 Put the recessed section of the hinge back into the hole and drive a ½ in. screw into each pilot hole.

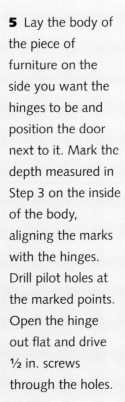

5 Lay the body of the piece of furniture on the side you want the hinges to be and position the door next to it. Mark the depth measured in Step 3 on the inside of the body, aligning the marks with the hinges. Drill pilot holes at the marked points. Open the hinge out flat and drive ½ in. screws through the holes.

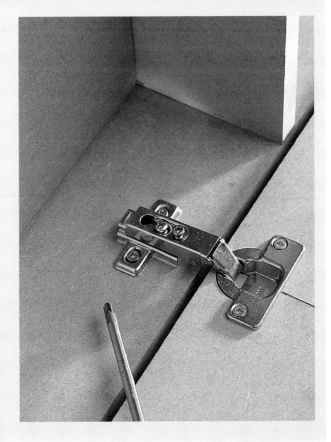

Utensil Rack

This handy little rack is designed to stand on your countertop and hold within easy reach the utensils and condiments that you need most often. If you do not have much space on your work surface, just drill holes through the back of the rack and use screws and wall plugs to attach it to the wall. Paint the rack to complement the color scheme in your own kitchen.

YOU WILL NEED

MDF

Back
• One piece
  15¾ x 9⅞ x ⅜ in.

Front
• One piece
  9⅞ x 4¼ x ⅜ in.

Rack
• One piece
  11 x 4 x ¾ in.

Base
• One piece
  9⅞ x 4½ x ⅜ in.

Sides
• Two pieces
  3¾ x 2¼ x ¾ in.

• Back, front, and rack
  templates on page 119
• Jigsaw
• Drill
• ³⁄₁₆ in. drill bit
• Countersink bit
• ¾ in. and 1 in. spade bits
• 2 in. hole saw
• Sanding block
• 120-grit sandpaper
• Wood glue
• Staple gun
• ⅝ in. staples
• Screwdriver

Screws
• 2: 1¼ in.

• Filling knife
• Filler
• Paintbrush
• Primer
• Satin paint

1 Enlarge the back, front, and rack templates by 300 percent and transfer them onto the appropriate pieces of MDF (see Template Techniques, page 112). Using the jigsaw, cut out the shapes (see Cutting with a Jigsaw, page 17). Predrill and countersink the marked ³⁄₁₆ in. holes in the back piece. Using the spade bits and hole saw, drill the marked holes in the rack piece (see Drilling and Countersinking, page 12). Using the jigsaw, cut the slot marked with the dotted line between two holes. Round off (see Finishing Techniques, page 110) both edges of the back piece between the marked points; below these points chamfer the back edges only. Round off both top edges and the front side edges of the front piece. Round off all edges of the rack piece and the edges of the drilled holes. In addition, round off the bottom edges of the base piece.

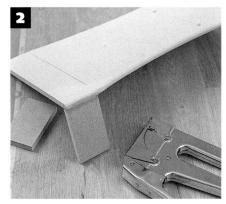

2 Glue and staple one side piece to one unrounded section of the back, firing staples through the back into the edge of the side piece (see Joining Two Pieces with Staples, page 28). Glue and staple the remaining side piece to the other side of the back in the same way.

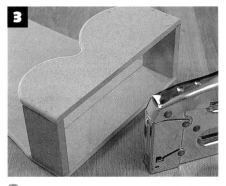

3 Glue and staple the unrounded side of the front piece to the ends of the side pieces, firing staples through the front into the edges of the side pieces.

4 Glue and staple the base to the edges of the front, back, and sides, firing staples through the base.

5 Glue and screw the rack to the back piece, driving screws through the predrilled holes in the back into the edge of the rack (see Joining Two

Pieces with Screws, page 13). Fill all screw and staple holes, sand the whole utensil rack, and prime it, then paint it with two coats of satin paint (see Finishing Techniques, page 110).

Liquor Cabinet

Taking inspiration from a traditional tallboy, this liquor cabinet will free up cupboard space in a traditional or contemporary style of kitchen. The top cupboard holds glasses of different sizes, while the bottom cupboard and integral wine rack store bottles and cocktail paraphernalia. Its slim shape also makes it suitable for a small kitchen.

YOU WILL NEED

Sides

MDF

- Three pieces
  55⅜ x 8 x ⅝ in.

Base and top

MDF

- Two pieces
  22 x 8 x ⅝ in.

Back

MDF

- One piece
  56⅝ x 22 x ¼ in.

Large shelves

MDF

- Four pieces
  16¾ x 8 x ⅝ in.

Small shelves

MDF

- Fourteen pieces
  8 x 3⅜ x ⅝ in.

Feet

Lumber

- Four pieces
  4¾ x 2⅜ x 1¾ in.

Doors

MDF

- One piece
  30½ x 17⅝ x ⅝ in.
- One piece
  26 x 17⅝ x ⅝ in.
- One piece
  23⅛ x 10¼ x ¼ in.

Glass

- One piece
  18½ x 10 x ⅛ in.

- Tape measure
- Pencil
- Drill
- 3/16 in., ⅛ in., and ½ in. drill bits
- Countersink bit
- Wood glue
- Screwdriver

Screws

- 80: 1⅜ in.
- 8: 1½ in.
- 32: ½ in.

- Staple gun
- ⅝ in. staples
- Template on page 115
- Jigsaw
- Router
- Rabbeting router bit
- Chisel
- Mallet
- Instant grab gap-filling adhesive
- Clear silicone sealant
- Four lay-on cabinet hinges
- Filling knife
- Filler
- Sanding block
- 120-grit sandpaper
- Paintbrush
- Primer
- Satin paint

1 Mark one short edge of a side piece (called A for ease of reference) as the bottom edge. From this edge, measure up 3¹¹⁄₁₆ in. and draw a line across the piece at this point. Measure up 4 in. from this line and draw another line. Continue measuring and drawing lines every 4 in. until you get to the top of the piece. The measurement above the last line will be 3¹¹⁄₁₆ in. Lay A on top of another side piece (B), aligning all edges, and predrill two 3/16 in. holes on each marked line, 2 in. from each edge. Drill through both pieces of MDF. Countersink the holes on A, then turn both pieces over together and countersink the holes on B (see Drilling and Countersinking, page 12).

2 Remove the side piece A and leave B countersunk-side up. Lay the unused side piece (C) on top of this, aligning all edges.

Working from the same bottom edge as marked on A in Step 1, measure up 14½ in. and draw a line across the piece at this point. Measure up 15½ in., 11½ in., and 7½ in. from this line and draw lines at all measured points. Predrill two 3/16 in. holes on each marked line, 2 in. from each edge. Drill right through both pieces of MDF. Countersink the holes on C, then turn both pieces over together and on B countersink only the holes you have just drilled.

3 Mark three lines across the width of the base piece. Mark one line ¼ in. from each short edge and the third line 4⁵⁄₁₆ in. from one short edge. Predrill and countersink two 3/16 in. holes on each line, positioning one hole 2 in. from each edge. Mark and drill the top piece in exactly the same way.

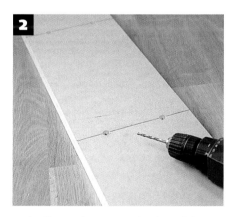

4 Butt the end of the base piece with only one drawn line against the bottom short edge of side piece C. Using a ⅛ in. drill bit, drill pilot holes through the predrilled holes in the base into the edges of C. Glue and screw the pieces together, driving 1⅜ in. screws through the predrilled holes into the pilot holes (see Joining Two Pieces with Screws, page 13). Fix the top piece to the other end of C in the same way.

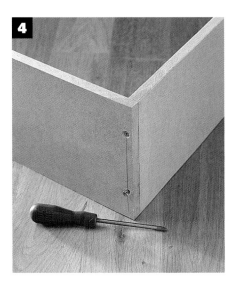

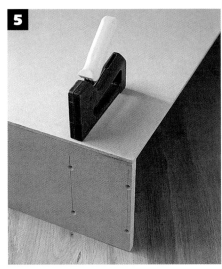

5 Turn the joined pieces over and lay the back on top of them. Glue and staple the pieces together, firing staples through the back piece into the edges of the side, base, and top pieces (see Joining Two Pieces with Staples, page 28).

6 Turn the unit back over so that it is lying on its back. Slot side piece B between the top and base pieces, aligning it with the next set of predrilled holes in the top and base pieces. Ensure that it is facing the right way around; the majority of the countersunk holes should be facing piece C. Drill pilot holes through the predrilled holes in the top and base pieces into the edges of B. Glue and screw the pieces together, driving 1⅜ in. screws through the predrilled holes into the pilot holes.

7 Working on the inside of the unit, measure up 14³⁄₁₆ in. from the base and draw a pencil line across the back. Sit a large shelf above this line, so that the edges of the shelf align with one of the sets of predrilled holes in the side pieces. Use a try square to check that the shelf is at right angles to the back and sides (see Using a Try Square, page 13). Drill pilot holes through the predrilled holes in the side pieces into the edges of the shelf. Glue and screw the pieces together, driving 1⅜ in. screws through the predrilled holes into the pilot holes. Measure up 14⅞ in. from this shelf and fix another large shelf in position in the same way. Fix the next large shelf 10⅞ in. above the previous one and the last large shelf 6⅞ in. above that one.

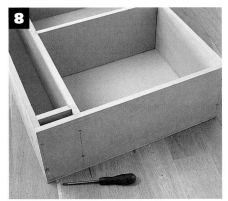

8 Slot side piece A between the top and base pieces, aligning it with the final set of predrilled holes. Ensure that it is facing the right way around; the majority of the countersunk holes should be facing outward. Use two of the small shelves as spacers to keep A in position while you drill pilot holes through the predrilled holes in the top and base pieces into the edges of A. Glue and screw the pieces together, driving 1⅜ in. screws through the predrilled holes into the pilot holes.

9 Slot a small shelf between side pieces A and B, aligning it with the lowest rows of predrilled holes. Use two other shelves as spacers to hold the shelf in position while you drill pilot holes through the predrilled holes in the side pieces into the edges of the shelf. Glue and screw the pieces together, driving 1⅜ in. screws through the predrilled holes into the pilot holes. Fix the other small shelves in position in the same way, aligning each one with a row of predrilled holes.

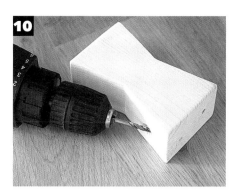

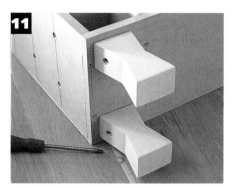

11 Glue and screw the feet to the base, positioning one foot ½ in. in from each corner. Drive 1½ in. screws through the predrilled holes into the base.

10 Enlarge the template by 200 percent and transfer it onto the four foot pieces of lumber (see Template Techniques, page 112). Using a jigsaw, cut out the shapes (see Cutting with a Jigsaw, page 17). Predrill and countersink ³⁄₁₆ in. holes at an angle through both sides of each foot, so that they emerge on the top of the foot, approximately ½ in. in from the edges.

customizing
THE CABINET

The shelves in the top cupboard are spaced to hold standard water glasses, wineglasses, and champagne flutes. However, consider the glasses you use and space the shelves accordingly. This cabinet was painted in vibrant dark blue to suit the contemporary kitchen that is its home, but a mellower color would make it equally suitable for a country-style kitchen. For a really rustic look, replace the glass panel with fine-mesh chicken wire stapled to the back of the door frame.

12 Draw a line 4 in. in from each edge of both thicker door pieces. Cut, rabbet, and chisel frames in both doors (see Making a Door Frame, page 49). Working on the larger door, run a line of instant grab adhesive around the inside of the rabbet and press the thin door piece into it. Wipe away excess adhesive on both sides with a damp cloth. Sand, prime, and paint the smaller door, then repeat the process with the clear sealant and piece of glass.

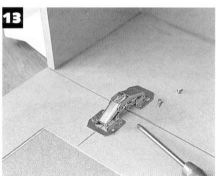

13 Using lay-on hinges, hang the larger door on the lower part of the cabinet and the smaller door on the upper part (see Hanging a Door Using Lay-on Hinges, page 23). The doors will meet over the edge of the third shelf down. Fill all screw holes, sand the unpainted parts of the cabinet, and prime them, then paint them with two coats of satin paint (see Finishing Techniques, page 110).

The Bedroom and Bathroom

Spare bed linen, out-of-season clothes, and accessories are often stored in a messy collection of bags and boxes. This chapter will help you store everything properly in the minimum space. And there are clever ideas for the bathroom, too—often the tiniest room in the house.

Nightstand

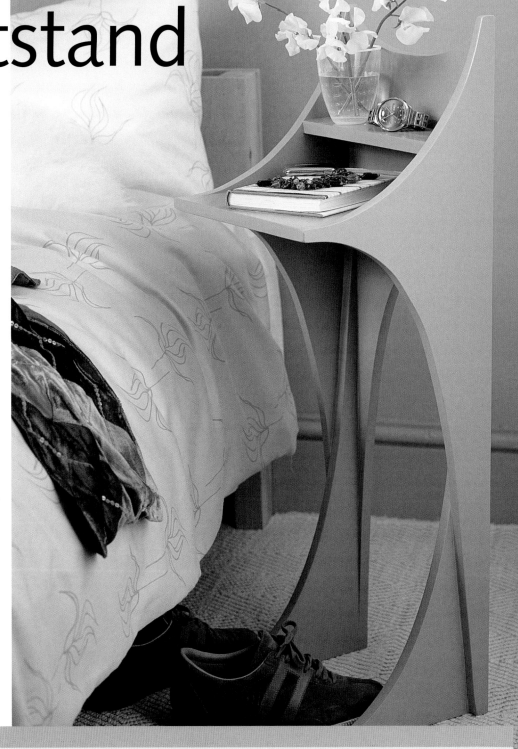

This is an ideal nightstand for a small bedroom, as its elegant curves take up little physical and visual space. It's also very easy and quick to make, requiring only careful cutting to get the best results.

YOU WILL NEED

MDF

Back
• One piece 33 x 11 x ⅝ in.

Sides
• One piece 33 x 11⅜ x ⅝ in.
• One piece 24 x 9¾ x ⅝ in.

Top
• One piece 9¾ x 9¾ x ⅝ in.

Shelf
• One piece 9¾ x 2¾ x ⅝ in.

• Back and two side templates on page 120
• Jigsaw

• Drill
• ³⁄₁₆ in. and ⅛ in. drill bits
• Countersink bit
• Wood glue
• Screwdriver

Screws
• 24: 1¼ in

• Filling knife
• Filler
• Sanding block
• 120-grit sandpaper
• Paintbrush
• Primer
• Satin paint

1 Enlarge the back template by 400 percent and transfer it onto the back piece of MDF (see Template Techniques, page 112). Using a jigsaw, cut out the shape (see Cutting with a Jigsaw, page 17). Predrill and countersink the marked ³⁄₁₆ in. holes (see Drilling and Countersinking, page 12).

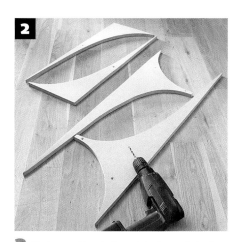

2 Enlarge the taller side template by 400 percent and transfer it twice onto the larger side piece of MDF. Lay the pieces top-to-toe, as shown. Repeat the process with the shorter side template and smaller piece of MDF. Using a jigsaw, cut out the shapes. Predrill and countersink the marked ³⁄₁₆ in. holes. Remember to countersink each pair of pieces on opposite sides.

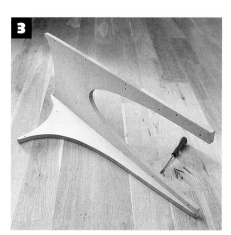

3 Butt the straight edge of one taller side piece up against one side of the back, aligning the tops of both pieces. Using a ⅛ in. drill bit, drill pilot holes through the predrilled holes in the back into the edge of the side piece. Glue and screw the two pieces together, driving screws through the predrilled holes into the pilot holes (see Joining Two Pieces with Screws, page 13).

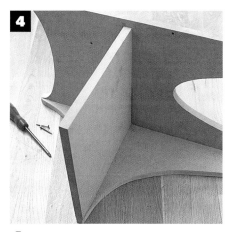

4 Butt the top piece against the side piece, aligning it with the predrilled holes in the side and back. Drill pilot holes through all the predrilled holes, and glue and screw the top in place, driving screws through the predrilled holes into the pilot holes.

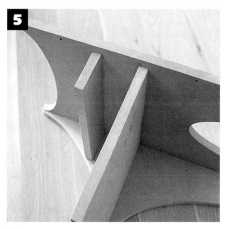

5 Butt the shelf piece against the side piece, aligning it with the predrilled holes in the side and back. Drill pilot holes through all the predrilled holes, and glue and screw the shelf in place, driving screws through the predrilled holes into the pilot holes. Attach the remaining taller side piece to the other side of the back piece (as in Step 3) and to the top and shelf, driving screws into the pilot holes.

6 Lay the shorter side pieces inside the taller ones, with the straight edges against the back. Align the straight bases with the bottom of the back. Drill pilot holes through the predrilled holes in the shorter side pieces and back. Glue and screw the pieces together, driving screws into the pilot holes. Fill all the screw holes, sand the nightstand and prime it, then paint it with two coats of satin paint (see Finishing Techniques, page 110).

Under-bed Drawer

The space under a bed offers excellent storage for all sorts of things, such as out-of-season clothes, bed linen, shoes, and even paperwork. However, if it isn't stored properly, you will spend a frustrating amount of time on your hands and knees trying to find the items you want. This drawer makes maximum use of available space, glides in and out smoothly, and can easily be adjusted to fit under any bed. The calico cover helps to keep stored items free from dust.

YOU WILL NEED

MDF

Base
- One piece 30 x 23½ x ⅝ in.

Front and back
- Two pieces 23½ x 6½ x ⅝ in.

Sides
- Two pieces 28¾ x 6½ x ⅝ in.

Castor housings
- Two pieces 28¾ x 2⅞ x ⅝ in.
- Two pieces 28¾ x 1⅝ x ⅝ in.

Cover

Calico
- One piece 30⅞ x 24⅜ in.
- Two pieces 30⅞ x 4¾ in.
- Two pieces 24⅜ x 4¾ in.

- Drill
- ³/₁₆ in., ⅜ in., and ⅛ in. drill bits
- Countersink bit
- Tape measure
- Pencil
- Jigsaw
- Screwdriver

Screws
- 60 x 1¼ in.
- 16: ½ in.
- Four fixed castors with 1⅞ in. diameter wheels, 2¼ in. fixing plates, and measuring 2⅝ in. from the bottom of the wheel to the fixing plate

- Filling knife
- Filler
- Sanding block
- 120-grit sandpaper
- Paintbrush
- Primer
- Satin paint
- Handle or length of thick cord
- Pinking shears
- Dressmaker's pins
- Sewing machine
- Sewing thread

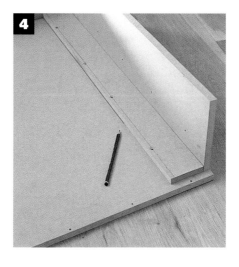

1 Predrill and countersink the following ³⁄₁₆ in. holes (see Drilling and Countersinking, page 12).

On the base piece, drill five holes along each side, ¼ in. in from the edge. Position one hole 2 in. from each corner, with three more spaced evenly between them. Drill five more holes along each long side, 3³⁄₁₆ in. in from the edge. Position the holes parallel to the existing ones.

On the front and back pieces, drill two holes along each short side, ¼ in. in from the edge. Position one hole 2 in. from each end. Drill one more hole on each short side, 1¾ in. in from the edge and 2 in. up from one long (bottom) edge.

On the side pieces, drill five holes, 2 in. up from one long (bottom) edge. Position one hole 2¾ in. from each end, with three more spaced evenly between them.

On the wide castor housing pieces, drill four holes along one long side, ¼ in. in from the edge. Position one hole 3½ in. from each end, with two more spaced evenly between them.

2 Using the ⅜ in. drill bit and the jigsaw, cut out four 2¼ in. square holes in the base (see Step 1 of Making a Door Frame, page 49). Position one hole in each corner, 4 in. in from the short side and ⅝ in. in from the long side.

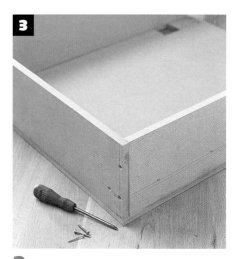

3 Align the long edge of the back piece with the four drilled holes nearest it, with a short side of the base. Using a ⅛ in. drill bit, drill pilot holes through the predrilled holes in the base into the edges of the side piece. Glue and screw the two pieces together, driving 1¼ in. screws through the predrilled holes into the pilot holes (see Joining Two Pieces with Screws, page 13). Attach the side pieces to the base in the same way, butting short edges up to the ends of the back piece. Drill pilot holes through the predrilled holes in the back piece into the edges of the side pieces and screw these together, too.

4 Lay a wide castor housing piece flat on the base, butting it up to one side piece. Draw a pencil line along the inner long side of the castor housing.

customizing
THE DRAWER

To make a longer or shorter drawer, simply alter the length of the side and both castor housing pieces. To make a taller or smaller drawer, alter the height of the side pieces. It is always best to leave a good-sized gap between the top of the drawer and the bottom of the bed, or the cover will snag when you pull it in and out. If you make several drawers, consider making the length equivalent to just under half the width of the bed. This way you can slide them under the bed from opposite sides and they will keep each other from going too far in.

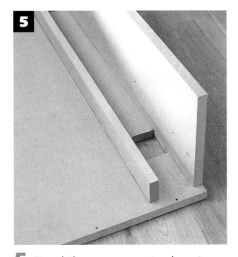

5 Stand the narrow castor housing piece inside the line. Drill pilot holes through the predrilled holes in the base and glue and screw the housing in place, driving 1¼ in. screws through the predrilled holes into the pilot holes.

7 Drill pilot holes and glue and screw the front piece to the base, sides, and castor housings, driving 1¼ in. screws through the predrilled holes into the pilot holes.

The calico cover

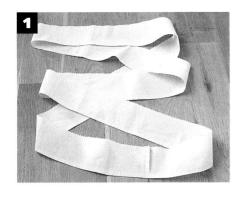

1 Pink all edges of the calico and take ⅜ in. seams throughout. Pin a short strip to each end of a long strip. Pin the remaining long strip to the free ends of the short ones to make a frame. Sew the pinned ends together. Turn under and sew a ⅜ in. hem around one edge.

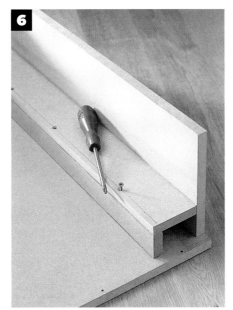

2 Pin the raw edge of the frame to rectangle of calico, matching the corners carefully. Sew the pieces together, pivoting at the corners. Turn the cover right-side out and press it.

6 Lay the wide castor housing piece on the edge of the narrow piece. Drill pilot holes through the predrilled holes in the wide housing into the edge of the narrow housing. Drill more pilot holes through the predrilled holes in the back and sides into the edges of the wide housing. Glue and screw the wide housing in place, driving 1¼ in. screws through the predrilled holes into the pilot holes. Repeat Steps 4–6 with the remaining castor housing pieces on the other side of the base.

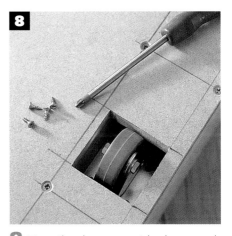

8 Turn the drawer upside down and put a castor into each cutout hole in the base, so that the fixing plates sit against the underside of the wide castor housings. Ensure that the castors are positioned centrally in the holes. Drive ½ in. screws straight through the holes in the castor fixing plates into the wide castor housing, making sure that the wheels are straight. Fill all screw holes, sand the whole drawer, and prime it, then paint it with two coats of satin paint (see Finishing Techniques, page 110). Either attach a handle to one end of the drawer, or as here, drill two holes in one end and thread a length of thick cord through, knotting it on the inside.

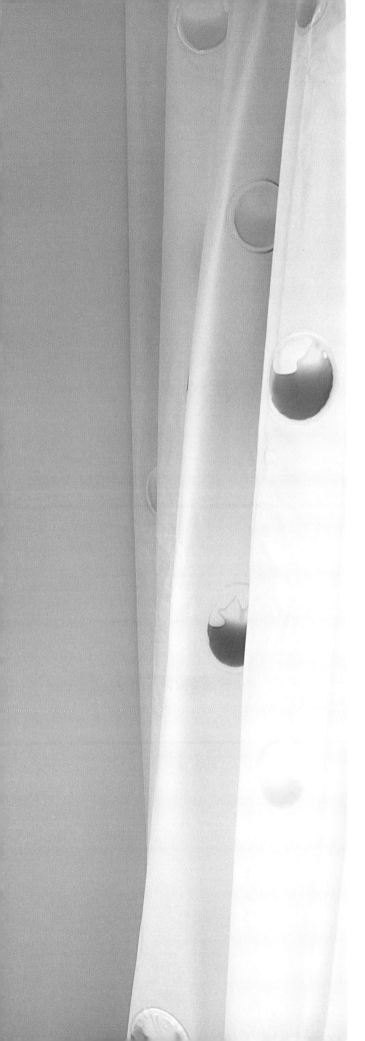

Mirror with Trays

A small bathroom can be a storage

nightmare of clutter precariously

balanced on the edges of the sink and

bath, all just waiting to be knocked over.

This design combines a mirror with

convenient trays for cosmetics and

bathroom paraphernalia, and it can easily

be adjusted to suit your own space.

YOU WILL NEED

MDF

Backboard
- One piece 27½ x 27½ x ¾ in.

Long narrow tray
- Two pieces 1¾ x 1⅜ x ⅜ in.
- One piece 9⅞ x 1¾ x ⅜ in.
- One piece 9⅞ x 1¾ x ¼ in.

Long wide tray
- Two pieces 2 x 1¾ x ⅜ in.
- One piece 9⅞ x 1¾ x ⅜ in.
- One piece 9⅞ x 2⅜ x ¼ in.

Small trays
- Four pieces 1¾ x 1½ x ⅜ in.
- Two pieces 4¹⁵⁄₁₆ x 1¾ x ⅜ in.
- Two pieces 4¹⁵⁄₁₆ x 1⅞ x ¼ in.

- Template on page 122
- Jigsaw
- Router
- Rounding-over and rabbeting router bits
- Chisel
- Mallet
- Drill
- ½ in., ³⁄₁₆ in., and ¹⁄₁₆ in. drill bits
- Countersink bit
- Wood glue
- Staple gun
- ⅝ in., ½ in., and 1¼ in. staples
- Small hammer
- Instant grab gap-filling adhesive
- 15 x 8⅝ in. mirror

- Damp cloth
- Filler knife
- Filler
- Sanding block
- 120-grit sandpaper
- Paintbrush
- Primer
- Satin paint
- Suitable wall fixings
- 4 screws with domed caps
- Screwdriver

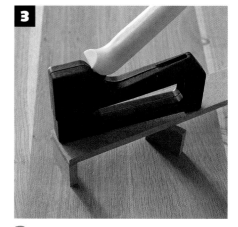

1 Enlarge the template by 500 percent and transfer it onto the backboard piece, transferring the tray position marks and the marked screw holes (see Template Techniques, page 112). Using the jigsaw, cut out the outer shape (see Cutting with a Jigsaw, page 17). Using the ½ in. drill bit and jigsaw, cut out the inner shape. Rabbet the back edges and chisel the corners (see Making a Door Frame, page 49). Using the rounding-over bit, rout a curve around the outer and inner edges of the shapes.

2 Predrill the marked ³⁄₁₆ in. holes. Predrill the marked ¹⁄₁₆ in. holes (see Drilling and Countersinking, page 12).

3 Make the long, narrow tray. Start by butting the edge of a small (side) piece up against the end of a long, thick (front) piece. Glue and staple the pieces together, firing ⅝ in. staples through the front into the edge of the side piece. Use the other side piece to support the end of the long piece while you staple. Glue and staple the other side piece in the same way.

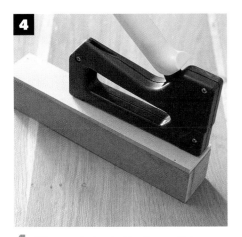

4 Glue and staple the long, thin (base) piece to the sides and front, using ½ in. staples. Make up the other three trays in the same way.

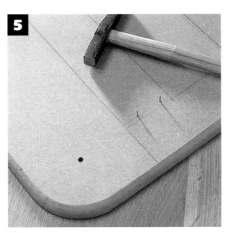

5 Break off sixteen individual 1¼ in. staples. Working from the back, hammer a staple through each ⅟₁₆ in. drilled hole, until they just protrude on the front.

6 Run a line of glue along the back edges of the long, narrow tray, and then lay it over the top set of staples, using the marks on the front of the backboard to ensure that it is level. Hammer the staples through into the edges of the tray. Fasten on the other trays in the same way, following the tray positions shown in the main picture and below.

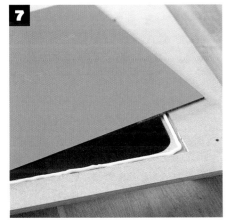

7 Run a line of instant grab adhesive around the inside of the rabbet and fit the mirror into it. Wipe away any excess adhesive with a damp cloth. Fill all staple holes, sand the MDF, and prime it, then paint it with two coats of satin paint (see Finishing Techniques, page 110). Use screws with domed caps and suitable wall fixings to attach the mirror to the wall, driving screws through the holes in the corners of the backboard (see Hanging Items on Walls, page 113).

customizing THE MIRROR

You can make the backboard any size and shape you want, and the trays can be positioned anywhere on it. Simply transfer the tray marks on the template to the appropriate positions. The trays can be up to 2¾ in. wide, though at this width it is better not to store heavy items in them. If you wish you could also attach hooks (see Letter Rack, Step 8, page 29) to the backboard to hang items such as bath brushes or wash cloths from.

Tipping
Drawers

YOU WILL NEED

MDF

Sides
- Two pieces
  42⅛ x 10⁷⁄₁₆ x ⅝ in.

End stops
- Six pieces 4 x 1 x ⅝ in.

Top and base
- Two pieces
  27½ x 10⁷⁄₁₆ x ⅝ in.

Back
- One piece 43⅜ x 27½ x ⅜ in.

Feet
- Four pieces 2 x 2 x ⅝ in.

Drawers
- Six pieces 11½ x 10 x ⅝ in.
- Three pieces 11⅝ x 26 x ⅝ in.
- Three pieces 11¼ x 26 x ⅝ in.

Sliding drawer
- Two pieces 26 x 6³⁄₁₆ x ⅝ in.
- Two pieces 9³⁄₁₆ x 6³⁄₁₆ x ⅝ in.
- One piece 26 x 10⁷⁄₁₆ x ¼ in.

- Drill
- ³⁄₁₆ in., ⅛ in., and ⁵⁄₁₆ in. drill bits
- Countersink bit
- Tape measure
- Pencil
- Wood glue
- Screwdriver

Screws
- 40: 1⅜ in.
- 16: 1 in.

- Template on page 122
- Jigsaw
- Plane
- Hammer
- Six ⁵⁄₁₆ in. chrome coach bolts, 2 in. long
- Twelve ⁵⁄₁₆ in. washers
- Twelve ⁵⁄₁₆ in. nuts
- Two spanners to fit nuts

- Staple gun
- ⅝ in. staples
- Filling knife
- Filler
- Sanding block
- 120-grit sandpaper
- Paintbrush
- Primer
- Satin paint
- Four door handles

Small items of clothing, such as scarves, socks, and underwear, don't fare well in conventional drawers. They slide to the back and tangle up. These tipping drawers, however, allow you to see all of the contents at once, making it easy to find the smallest thing. The sliding drawer in the base will hold folded items.

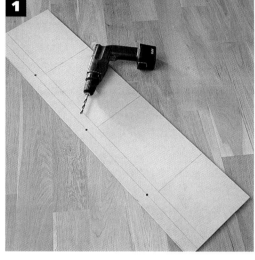

1 On one side piece, predrill (but do not countersink) three ⁵⁄₁₆ in. holes, 1⁵⁄₁₆ in. from one long (front) side (see Drilling and Countersinking, page 12). Position one hole 10 in., another hole 21⅞ in., and the third 33¾ in. from one short (top) side. Draw a pencil line 2⁹⁄₁₆ in. in from the front side. Draw three horizontal lines from this line across to the other side, positioning them 10⅝ in., 22½ in., and 34⅜ in. from the top side.

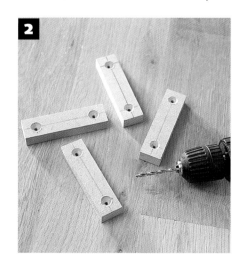

2 Predrill and countersink two ³⁄₁₆ in. holes in each of the end stop pieces. Position one hole 1 in. from each end and centrally across the width.

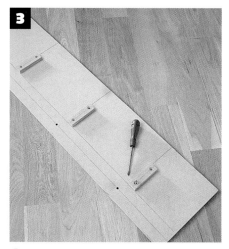

3 Position one end stop below each horizontal line, butting a short end up to the vertical line. Using a ⅛ in. drill bit, drill pilot holes through the predrilled holes in the end stops into the side piece. Glue and screw the pieces together, driving 1 in. screws through the predrilled holes into the pilot holes (see Joining Two Pieces with Screws, page 13). Following Steps 1–3, make up the other side piece as a mirror image of the first.

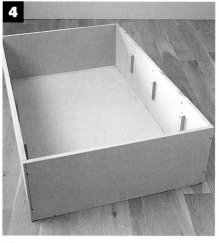

4 Using the side, top, base, and back pieces, and 1⅜ in. screws, make up a cabinet, following Steps 1–5 of Basic Cupboard (see page 20). However, instead of drilling five holes in each long side of the top and base pieces, drill two holes in each short side of the top and base pieces, positioning one hole 2 in. from each edge. Do not drill holes for shelves.

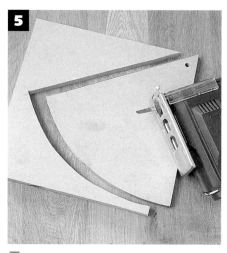

5 Enlarge the template by 400 percent and transfer it onto the six small drawer pieces (see Template Techniques, page 112). Using a jigsaw, cut out the side shapes (see Cutting with a Jigsaw, page 17). Predrill the marked 5⁄16 in. hole.

6 On the six larger drawer pieces, draw a line 5⁄16 in. in from one long edge. Use a plane to chamfer the edge up to the drawn line, thus making an angled edge.

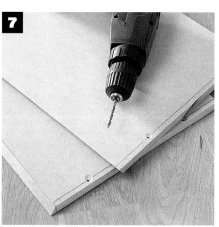

7 On both short sides of the six larger drawer pieces, draw a line ¼ in. in from the edge. Predrill and countersink two 3⁄16 in. holes on each line, positioning one hole 2½ in. from each end. On the three largest (front) drawer pieces, countersink the holes on the chamfered sides. On the three remaining (back) pieces, countersink the holes on the side that is not chamfered.

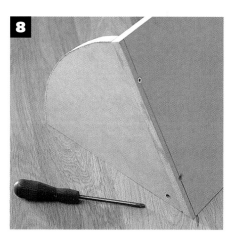

8 Butt one straight edge of a side piece against one short end of a back piece. The chamfered edge of the back piece must be flush with the other straight edge of the side piece. Drill pilot holes through the predrilled holes in the back piece into the edges of the side piece. Glue and screw the pieces together, driving 1⅜ in. screws into the pilot holes. Attach another side piece to the other end of the back piece in the same way.

9 Butt a front piece against the free edges of the side pieces, with the chamfered edge overlapping the chamfered edge of the back piece. Pilot-drill, glue, and screw the pieces together. Make up two more drawers the same way.

10 Slide a bolt into each hole in the cabinet. Slip washers onto the bolts then screw on nuts. Tighten the nuts until the square part of the bolt heads sink into the MDF. Remove the nuts and washers and hammer the bolts out of the holes.

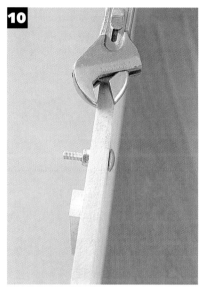

As the tipping drawers are much slimmer than a standard chest of drawers, this is a good storage solution for a small bedroom.

11 Put a bolt into each of the top holes, with the ends just protruding into the cabinet. Slip a washer onto both bolts. Slide a drawer into the cabinet, aligning the holes in the drawer sides

with the bolts. Hammer the bolts through into the drawer. Ensure that the heads of the bolts sit in the depression made in Step 10. Slide another washer onto each bolt, then tighten up a nut. Screw a second nut onto each bolt, and using a spanner on both nuts, tighten them against each other to lock them off. Fit the other drawers the same way.

12 Predrill and countersink two ³⁄₁₆ in. holes in the short edges of the sliding drawer front and back pieces, ¼ in. in from the edge. Position one hole 1¼ in. in from

each long edge. Make up a frame following Step 2 of Basic Bookcase (see page 10). Lay the back over the frame and glue and staple it in place (see Joining Two Pieces with Staples, page 28). Slide the drawer into the bottom of the cabinet. Fill all screw holes, sand and prime the unit, then paint it with two coats of satin paint (see Finishing Techniques, page 110). Attach a handle to each drawer.

Bathroom Cabinet

Compact in size, but offering plenty of storage, this curvaceous cabinet will hold bathroom accessories and support hand towels on the integrated rail.

YOU WILL NEED

Front

MDF

- One piece 20 x 12½ x ⅝ in.

Mirror

- One piece 16 x 8⅝ in.

Sides

MDF

- Two pieces 23½ x 7⅛ x ⅝ in.

Top and base

MDF

- Two pieces 8¼ x 7⅛ x ⅝ in.

Shelf

MDF

- One piece 8¼ x 5 x ⅝ in.

Back

MDF

- One piece 15¾ x 9½ x ¼ in.

Rail

Dowel

- One length 12¼ x ¾ in.

- Front and side templates on page 121
- Jigsaw

- Drill
- ½ in., ³⁄₁₆ in., and ⅛ in. drill bits
- Countersink bit
- ¾ in. spade bit
- Wood glue
- Screwdriver

Screws

- 12: 1 in.
- 10: ¾ in.
- 12: ½ in., ⅛ in. thick
- 4: suitable for wall fixings

- Tape measure
- Pencil
- 12¾ x ¾ in. length of piano hinge
- Door handle
- Filling knife
- Filler
- Sanding block
- 120-grit sandpaper
- Paintbrush
- Primer
- Satin paint
- Instant grab gap-filling adhesive
- Magnetic door catch
- Epoxy adhesive
- Suitable wall fixings

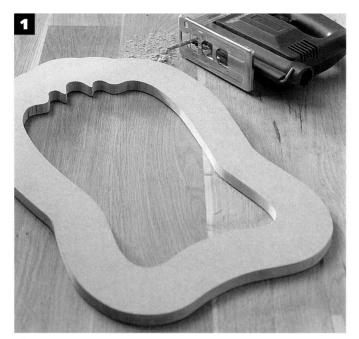

1 Enlarge the front template by 333 percent and transfer it onto the front piece (see Template Techniques, page 112). Using a jigsaw, cut out the outer shape (see Cutting with a Jigsaw, page 17). Using a ½ in. drill bit and jigsaw, cut out the inner shape. The principle is exactly the same as for cutting out a rectangle, but cut along the curved internal lines (see Steps 1–2 of Making a Door Frame, page 49).

2 Enlarge the side templates by 333 percent and transfer them onto the side pieces of MDF. Using a jigsaw, cut out the shapes. Predrill and countersink the marked ³⁄₁₆ in. holes. Drill the marked ¾ in. holes (see Drilling and Countersinking, page 12).

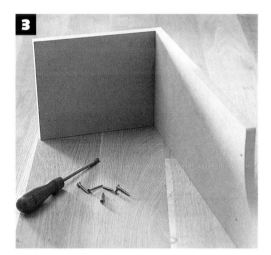

3 Butt the edge of the top piece against the square end of one side piece. Using a ⅛ in. drill bit, drill pilot holes through the predrilled holes in the side into the edge of the top piece. Glue and screw the two pieces together, driving 1¼ in. screws through the predrilled holes into the piloted holes (see Joining Two Pieces with Screws, page 13).

4 Attach the shelf piece and the base piece to the side piece in the same way, aligning the ends with the predrilled holes in the side piece.

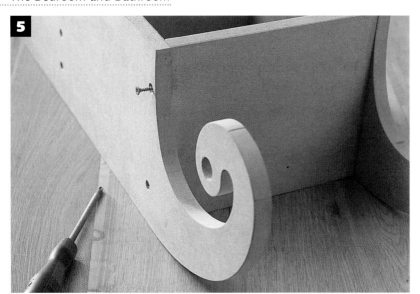

5 Drill pilot holes and glue and screw the other side piece to the free ends of the top, shelf, and base pieces, aligning them with the predrilled holes, as before.

7 Lay the cabinet on its right-hand side. Lay the hinge centrally along the outside of the left-hand side. The knuckle of the hinge faces in and protrudes beyond the edge of the MDF, as shown. Screw the hinge to the cabinet, driving ½ in. screws through the holes.

8 Lay the door facedown and lay the body of the cabinet facedown on top of it, positioning it so that all four corners are within the door. Draw a pencil line around the edges of the cabinet onto the door frame.

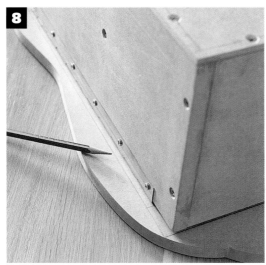

6 Predrill and countersink ten ³⁄₁₆ in. holes in the back piece, ¼ in. in from the edge. On the short sides, position one hole 2 in. from each end. On the long sides, position one hole 2 in. from each end with one more centrally between them. Lay the cabinet facedown and position the back over it. Drill pilot holes through the predrilled holes into the edges of the side, top, and base pieces. Glue and screw the back in place, driving ¾ in. screws through the predrilled holes into the pilot holes.

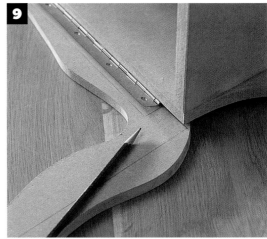

9 Leaving the door in position, lay the cabinet on the hinge side, positioning it so that the edge of the cabinet is against the pencil line drawn in Step 8. Open the hinge out so that it lies flat on the door and draw a pencil line around it. Screw the hinge to the door within the marked line, driving ½ in. screws through the holes.

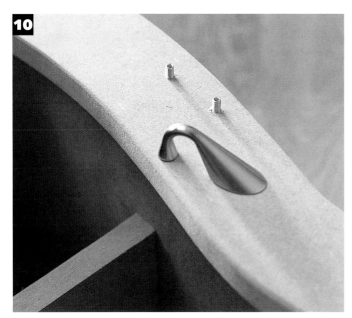

10 Fasten the door handle to the right-hand side of the door, drilling any necessary holes outside the pencil lines drawn on the back. Once the holes are drilled, remove the handle again before painting the cabinet.

11 Push the dowel through both ¾ in. holes in the bottom of the sides, positioning it centrally. Pull it back slightly and spread a little glue around it at the points where it was inside the drilled holes. Push the dowel back into place. Fill all screw holes, sand the whole cabinet, and prime it, then paint it with two coats of satin paint (see Finishing Techniques, page 110).

customizing
THE CABINET

The width of the cabinet can easily be adjusted by altering the lengths of the top, base, shelf, and dowel pieces, and the width of the back. Within the cabinet you can position shelves at different heights; just transfer the screw holes marked on the template to the appropriate positions.

12 When the paint is dry, run a line of adhesive around the edge of the mirror and press it facedown onto the back of the door, making sure that it covers all of the cutout shape. Wipe away any excess adhesive with a damp cloth. Glue the metal plate of the door catch to the back of the mirror with epoxy adhesive. Screw the other half of the catch to the inside of the cabinet, following the manufacturer's instructions and aligning it with the plate. Replace the door handle. Drill a hole in each corner of the back of the cabinet and use screws and suitable wall fixings to attach the mirror to the wall through these holes (see Hanging Items on Walls, page 113).

The
Office

A home office is often stolen space in a room that also serves another purpose. Office equipment should, therefore, be housed in a piece of furniture that suits the room and allows as many items as possible to be easily tided away or screened off.

Corner Desk

Even if you don't work at home, there is still paperwork to do, which tends to accumulate in messy piles until it finally gets tackled on the kitchen table. This compact corner desk provides a home for all this paper and takes up minimum space in a living room or bedroom. If you do use a computer, you will find the top large enough to hold one, and the flap is a perfect keyboard rest.

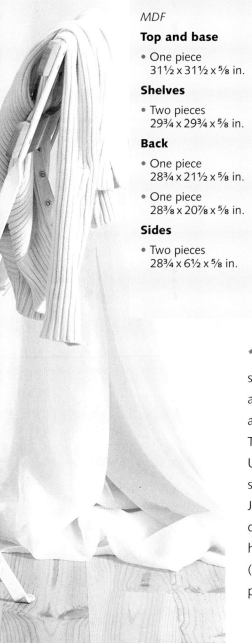

YOU WILL NEED

MDF

Top and base
- One piece
  31½ x 31½ x ⅝ in.

Shelves
- Two pieces
  29¾ x 29¾ x ⅝ in.

Back
- One piece
  28¾ x 21½ x ⅝ in.
- One piece
  28⅜ x 20⅞ x ⅝ in.

Sides
- Two pieces
  28¾ x 6½ x ⅝ in.

Flap
- One piece
  30¹³⁄₃₂ x 6 x ⅝ in.

Doors
- Two pieces
  22¾ x 15³⁄₁₆ x ⅝ in.

Feet
- Three pieces
  1 x 1 x ⅝ in.

- Top, base and shelf templates on page 123
- Jigsaw
- Drill
- ³⁄₁₆ in. and ⅛ in. drill bits

- Countersink bit
- Tape measure
- Pencil
- Plane
- Wood glue
- Screwdriver

Screws
- 46: 1⅜ in.
- 8: 1 in.
- 3: ¾ in.
- Enough to attach hinges, piano hinge, and stays: ½ in.

- 29 in. piano hinge
- Stays
- Plunge cutter
- Four recessed cabinet hinges
- Filling knife
- Filler
- Sanding block
- 120-grit sandpaper
- Paintbrush
- Primer
- Satin paint
- Three door handles

1 Enlarge the top, base, and shelf templates by 667 percent and transfer them onto the appropriate pieces of MDF (see Template Techniques, page 112). Using the jigsaw, cut out the shapes (see Cutting with a Jigsaw, page 17). Predrill and countersink the marked ³⁄₁₆ in. holes in the top and base (see Drilling and Countersinking, page 12).

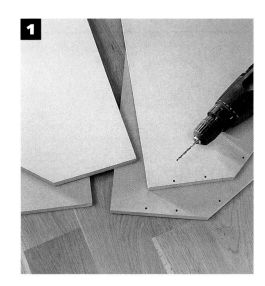

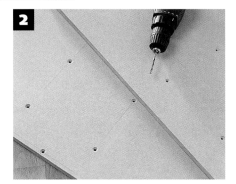

2 In the larger back piece, predrill and countersink four ³⁄₁₆ in. holes down one long side, ¼ in. in from the edge. Position one hole 2 in. from each corner, with two holes spaced evenly between them. Draw pencil lines across both back pieces 15¼ in. and 22⁷⁄₁₆ in. up from one short side. Predrill and countersink four ³⁄₁₆ in. holes along each line. Position one hole 2¾ in. from each end, with two holes spaced evenly between them.

4 Position the larger back piece on one long edge of the base, aligning the drilled edge of the back with the corner of the base. Drill pilot holes through the predrilled holes in the base piece into the edges of the back piece. Glue and screw the two pieces together, driving 1³⁄₈ in. screws through the predrilled holes into the pilot holes (see Joining Two Pieces with Screws, page 13).

5 Stand the smaller back piece on the base, butting one long side up to the drilled edge of the larger back piece. Drill pilot holes through the predrilled holes in the base and larger back piece, then glue and screw the pieces together, driving 1³⁄₈ in. screws through the predrilled holes into the pilot holes.

3 Draw a line ⁷⁄₁₆ in. in from one long edge on both side pieces. Using the plane, chamfer up to the line to make an angle of 45°. Draw pencil lines across both pieces 15¼ in. and 22⁷⁄₁₆ in. up from one short side. Predrill and countersink one ³⁄₁₆ in. hole on each line, 2¾ in. from the square edge.

6 Stand one side piece on the base, butting the planed edge against the square edge of a back piece. Drill pilot holes through the predrilled holes in the base, then glue and screw the side piece to the base, driving 1³⁄₈ in. screws through the predrilled holes into the pilot holes. Predrill and countersink four holes in the angled edge of the side piece, ³⁄₈ in. in from the edge. Drill pilot holes through these holes into the edge of the back piece. Glue and screw the side piece to the back piece, driving 1 in. screws through the predrilled holes into the pilot holes. Repeat with the other side piece on the other side of the unit.

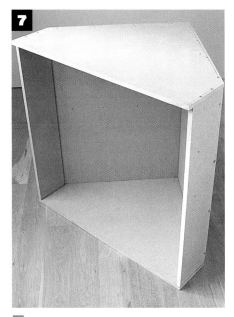

7 Lay the top piece on top of the back and sides. Glue and screw the top to the back and sides, driving 1⅜ in. screws through the predrilled holes in the top.

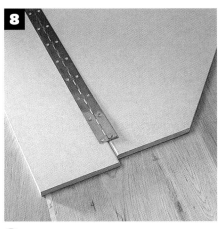

8 Using the plane, chamfer the top edge of the straight (front) side of one shelf. The chamfer must be enough to accommodate the knuckle of the piano hinge. Do the same on one long edge of the flap, so that when the two edges are butted up together, the hinge lies flat across them.

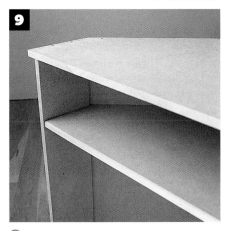

9 Position the chamfered shelf in the unit, aligning it with the top row of predrilled holes in the sides and backs and ensuring that the chamfer is on the top. Drill pilot holes through the predrilled holes in the back and sides, and glue and screw the shelf in place, driving 1⅜ in. screws through the predrilled holes into the pilot holes. Fix the second shelf in position in the same way, aligning it with the lower holes. Attach a foot to the corners of the base, following Step 8 of Basic Blanket Box (see page 18).

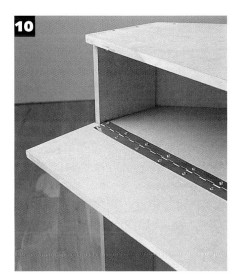

10 Center the hinge on the chamfered edge of the flap, with the knuckle of the hinge against the chamfer. Drill pilot holes through the holes in the hinge and screw the hinge to the flap, driving ½ in. screws into the pilot holes. Screw the other side of the hinge to the front of the chamfered shelf in the same way.

11 Attach a stay on either side of the unit, using ½ in. screws and following the manufacturer's instructions. Ensure that the flap is level.

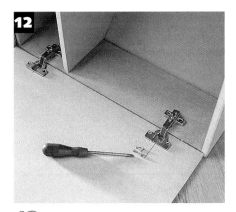

12 Hang the doors using recessed hinges (see Hanging a Door Using Recessed Hinges, page 59). Draw the initial pencil line 4 in. from each end of the doors. Fill all screw holes, sand the desk, and prime it, then paint it with two coats of satin paint (see Finishing Techniques, page 110). Attach the handles to the doors and flap.

Computer Desk

Inspired by the design of a classic rolltop desk, this computer desk provides a home for modern technology, and yet it will sit happily in a traditionally styled home. A deep cupboard holds the CPU and peripherals, holes in the back allow easy cord access, and the top is wide enough for a monitor and keyboard. The high sides partially screen the desktop and help confine the clutter.

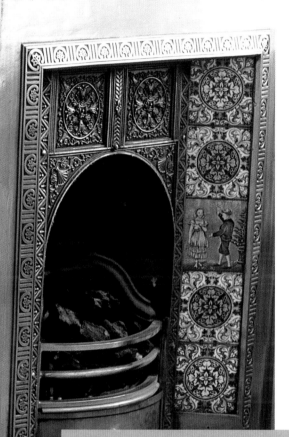

YOU WILL NEED

MDF

Desk sides
- Two pieces 47½ x 24 x ¾ in.

Desk back
- One piece 40¾ x 40¾ x ⅜ in.

Desktop
- One piece 39½ x 24 x ¾ in.

Cupboard sides
- Two pieces 29½ x 21⅝ x ⅝ in.

Cupboard top, base, and shelf
- Three pieces 12 x 21⅝ x ⅝ in.

Cupboard back
- One piece 29⅛ x 13 x ⅜ in.

Cupboard door
- One piece 29⅜ x 13 x ⅝ in.

- Template on page 125
- Jigsaw
- Drill
- ³⁄₁₆ in. and ⅛ in. drill bits
- Countersink bit
- Tape measure
- Pencil
- Wood glue
- Screwdriver

Screws
- 29: 2 in.
- 18: 1⅜ in.
- 12: 1 in.
- 16: ½ in.

- Two lay-on cabinet hinges
- Filling knife
- Filler
- Sanding block
- 120-grit sandpaper
- Paintbrush
- Primer
- Satin paint
- Door handle

1 Enlarge the template by 667 percent and transfer it onto the two side pieces (see Template Techniques, page 112). Using a jigsaw, cut out the shapes (see Cutting with a Jigsaw, page 17). Predrill and countersink the marked ³⁄₁₆ in. holes (see Drilling and Countersinking, page 12).

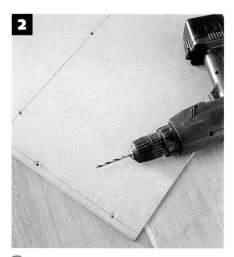

2 Predrill and countersink seven ³⁄₁₆ in. holes on both long sides of the back, ¼ in. in from the edge. Position one hole 2 in. from each end, with five more holes spaced evenly between them. Draw a line 29⅞ in. from one short (lower) edge. Predrill and countersink five holes on the line, positioning one hole 2 in. from each end, one hole 12⅝ in. from each end and one more hole centrally.

3 Decide on which side of the desk you want the cupboard to be, and using a jigsaw, cut an arc 2⅜ in. deep and 8 in. long in one long side of the desktop piece to allow cables to go through. The arc should be 2½ in. from one short side.

4 Butt one short edge of the desktop against the row of drilled holes in one side piece. Using a ⅛ in. drill bit, drill pilot holes through the predrilled holes in the side piece into the edge of the desktop. Glue and screw the two pieces together, driving 2 in. screws through the predrilled holes into the pilot holes (see Joining Two Pieces with Screws, page 13).

5 Attach the other side piece to the other end of the desktop in the same way.

6 Lay the desk facedown and lay the back piece on top of it, aligning the bases of the back and sides. Drill pilot holes through the predrilled holes in the back piece into the edge of the desktop and side pieces. Glue and screw the pieces together, driving 2 in. screws through the predrilled holes into the pilot holes.

7 Draw lines across both cupboard side pieces ¼ in. and 9½ in. from one short (top) side, and another line ¾ in. from the other short (bottom) side. Predrill and countersink three ³⁄₁₆ in. holes on each line, positioning one hole 2 in. from each end, with one more hole centrally between them.

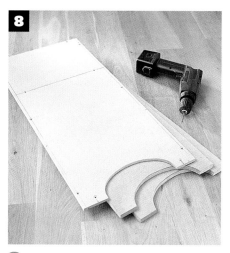

8 On one short side of the top, shelf, and back pieces, draw arcs to match the one in the desktop, starting 2 in. from each side. Using a jigsaw, cut out the shapes. Predrill and countersink ³⁄₁₆ in. holes in the back piece, ¼ in. in from the edges. On the long sides position one hole 2 in. from each end, with one hole between them. On the short sides position one hole 1½ in. from each end. Draw a horizontal line 9½ in. from the top and position one hole 1½ in. from each end.

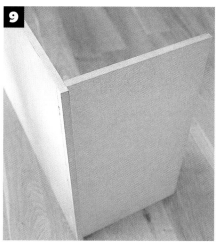

9 Butt one long edge of the base piece against the lower end of a side piece, aligning it with the row of predrilled holes. Drill pilot holes through the predrilled holes in the side piece into the edge of the base piece. Glue and screw the pieces together, driving 1⅜ in. screws through the predrilled holes into the pilot holes.

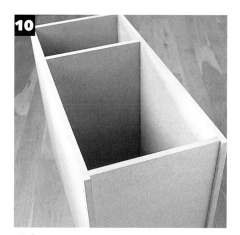

10 Attach the top and shelf pieces to the side piece in the same way, aligning them with the rows of predrilled holes. Attach the other side piece to the free ends of the top, shelf, and base pieces as in Step 9.

11 Lay the back piece on the cupboard, with the arc at the bottom. Drill pilot holes through the predrilled holes in the back piece into the edges of the base, top, side, and shelf pieces. Glue and screw the pieces together, driving 1 in. screws through the predrilled holes into the pilot holes.

12 Hang the door using lay-on hinges (see Hanging a Door Using Lay-on Hinges, page 23). Fill all screw holes, sand the desk and cupboard, and prime them, then paint them with two coats of satin paint (see Finishing Techniques, page 110). Attach the handle.

Workstation

A teenager's bedroom needs to look good, have space to work in, and have room for the inevitable clutter. The contemporary, curving lines of this desk will please the style-conscious, and the generous work surface will hold all sorts of things—including a computer—and still have room for homework.

YOU WILL NEED

MDF

Sides
- Two pieces
  38 x 21½ x ¾ in.

Back
- One piece 48 x 48 x ¾ in.

Flap
- One piece 48 x 8½ x ¾ in.

Top
- One piece 46½ x 38 x ¾ in.

- Side, back, and flap
  templates on pages 124–125
- Jigsaw
- Drill
- ³⁄₁₆ in. and ⅛ in. drill bits
- Countersink bit
- Router
- Rounding-over router bit

- Wood glue
- Screwdriver

Screws
- 25: 2 in.
- Enough for hinge and
  stays: ½ in.

- Tape measure
- Two stays
- 45½ in. piano hinge
- Filling knife
- Filler
- Sanding block
- 120-grit sandpaper
- Paintbrush
- Primer
- Satin paint

1 Enlarge the side, back, and flap templates by 714 percent and transfer them onto the pieces of MDF (see Template Techniques, page 112). Using a jigsaw, cut out the shapes (see Cutting with a Jigsaw, page 17). Predrill and countersink the marked ³⁄₁₆ in. holes: on the side pieces, countersink the holes on the same side of both pieces, not on opposite sides as is usual (see Drilling and Countersinking, page 13). Using the rounding-over bit, rout a curve around the edges marked on the template (see Step 1 of Mirror with Trays, page 74).

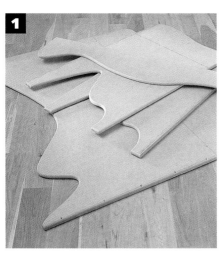

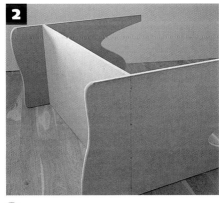

2 Butt one short edge of the top piece against the row of drilled holes in one side piece. Drill pilot holes through the predrilled holes in the side piece into the edges of the top piece. Glue and screw the pieces together, driving 2 in. screws through the predrilled holes into the pilot holes (see Joining Two Pieces with Screws, page 13). Attach the other side piece to the other end of the top piece in the same way. As the sides are countersunk on the same face, they do not mirror one another, adding to the organic feel.

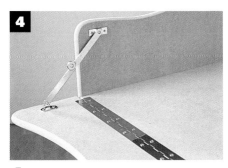

4 Attach the flap to the front of the top using the piano hinge and then attach the stays, following Steps 8, 10, and 11 of Corner Desk (see page 88). Fill all screw holes, sand the whole desk, and prime it, then paint it with two coats of satin paint (see Finishing Techniques, page 110).

3 Lay the desk facedown and lay the back piece on top of it, aligning the bases of the back and sides. Drill pilot holes through the predrilled holes in the back piece into the edges of the top and side pieces. Glue and screw the pieces together, driving 2 in. screws through the predrilled holes into the pilot holes.

Tidying up the room just got a bit easier—fold up the front flap of the desk to instantly conceal clutter.

The Garden

Even the smallest, easiest-to-maintain garden needs some equipment to keep it looking good all year round. Versatile storage solutions that hold as much as possible in the smallest space are the answer here.

Garden Box

This box was designed to store folding deckchairs and garden tools, but it is easy to adapt the measurements to suit your own garden and the items you want to store. If the box is going to be visible, consider decorating the lid to turn it into an attractive feature in the garden.

YOU WILL NEED

Sides
Marine plywood
- Two pieces 29¾ x 21⅝ x ¾ in.

Back
Marine plywood
- One piece 54⁵⁄₁₆ x 29¼ x ¾ in.

Base
Marine plywood
- One piece 55¹³⁄₁₆ x 21⅝ x ½ in.

Front
Marine plywood
- One piece 54⁵⁄₁₆ x 22⅝ x ¾ in.

Feet
Marine plywood
- Six pieces 2⅜ x 2⅜ x ¼ in.

Lid
Marine plywood
- One piece 57½ x 25¼ x ¾ in.
- One piece 25¼ x 7 x ¾ in.
- Two pieces 56 x 1 x ¾ in.

Dowel
- One length 62¾ x 1 in.
- Two lengths 1½ x ¼ in.

- Box side and lid side templates on page 126
- Jigsaw
- Drill
- ³⁄₁₆ in., ⅛ in., and ¼ in. drill bits
- Countersink bit
- 1¼ in. hole saw

- Wood glue
- Screwdriver
Screws
- 70: 1½ in.

- Staple gun
- ⅝ in. staples
- ½ in. spade bit
- Filling knife
- Filler
- Sanding block
- 120-grit sandpaper
- Paintbrush
- Exterior primer
- Exterior paint

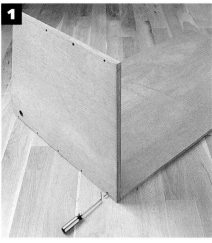

1 Enlarge the box side template by 500 percent and transfer it onto the two side pieces (see Template Techniques, page 112). Using the jigsaw, cut out the shapes (see Cutting with a Jigsaw, page 17). Predrill and countersink the marked ³⁄₁₆ in. holes and using the hole saw, drill the marked 1¼ in. hole (see Drilling and Countersinking, page 12). Butt one short edge of the back piece against the long side of one side piece. Using a ⅛ in. drill bit, drill pilot holes through the predrilled holes in the side piece into the edges of the back piece. Glue and screw the two pieces together, driving screws through the predrilled holes into the pilot holes (see Joining Two Pieces with Screws, page 13).

2 Predrill ³⁄₁₆ in. holes along each side of the base piece, ½ in. in from the edge. On the long sides, position one hole 2 in. from each end, with six more holes spaced evenly between them. On the short sides position one hole 2 in. from each end, with two more holes spaced evenly between them. Drill pilot holes through the predrilled holes in the base piece into the edges of the side and back pieces. Glue and screw the pieces together, driving screws through the predrilled holes into the pilot holes.

customizing
THE BOX

The lid of the box can be decorated in many ways—with a paint effect, stenciled patterns, or a stamped design. The lid of this box was given a verdigris effect using a simple technique. Paint the lid with a coat of exterior varnish, and while this is still wet, sprinkle copper powder all over it. Leave the varnish to dry. Blow off any excess powder. Spray patinating fluid unevenly over the copper and leave it for the time stated on the packaging. The fluid will react with the copper powder and produce a verdigris effect. Once the reaction is complete, paint the whole lid with a second coat of exterior varnish. Copper powder and patinating fluid are available from craft stores.

3 Turn the box over so that it is standing on the base. Butt the edge of the front piece up to the side piece and ensure that it is flush with the edge of the base. Drill pilot holes through the predrilled holes in the side piece into the edge of the front piece. Glue and screw the pieces together, driving screws through the predrilled holes into the pilot

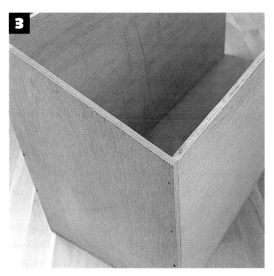

holes. Turn the box onto its back and pilot drill and drive screws through the predrilled holes in the base into the long edge of the front. Butt the remaining side piece up to the ends of the front and back pieces, ensuring that it is flush with the base. Drill pilot holes through the predrilled holes in the side piece into the edges of the front and back pieces. Glue and screw the pieces together, driving screws through the predrilled holes into the pilot holes. Turn the box onto its back and pilot drill and drive screws through the predrilled holes in the base into the edge of the side.

4 Glue and staple a foot to each corner of the base, 1 in. in from the corner (see Joining Two Pieces with Staples, page 13). Staple another foot to the center front and back of the base, 1 in. in from the edge. Using the spade bit, drill a drainage hole close to each corner of the base of the box.

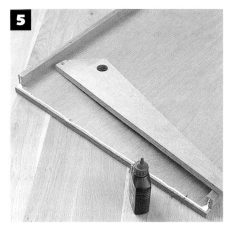

5 Make up the lid using the same principles as the box, enlarging the lid side template by the same percentage. Predrill and countersink holes along each side of the large lid piece, ½ in. in from the edge. On the long sides position one hole 2 in. from each end, with six more spaced evenly between them. On the short sides position one hole 2 in. from each end, with two more spaced evenly between them.

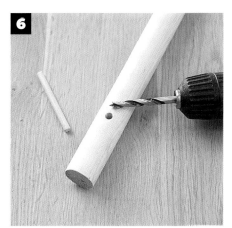

6 Place the lid on the box, aligning the 1¼ in. holes. Thread the long dowel through all the holes (you may find it easier to open the lid a little to do this). Ensure that an equal amount of dowel protrudes at each end of the box. Mark the dowel ⅛ in. out from the side of the lid on each side. Remove the dowel and drill two ¼ in. holes through it at the marked points.

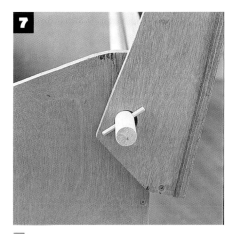

7 Thread the dowel back through the box and lid. Spread a little glue around the middle of each of the short lengths of dowel and push one through each drilled hole. Fill all screw holes, sand the whole box, and prime it, then paint it with two coats of exterior paint (see Finishing Techniques, page 110).

Hose Storage

The garden hose reels sold in stores are almost always made of plastic, and while they are functional, they are usually unattractive. This hose reel can be painted to suit its setting and as well as holding your hose, it also has a rack and pockets to store the various attachments needed for watering different parts of the garden.

1 Enlarge the template by 400 percent and transfer it twice onto the smaller roof piece (see Template Techniques, page 112). Using a jigsaw, cut out the pieces (see Cutting with a Jigsaw, page 17).

YOU WILL NEED

Roof

Marine plywood

- One piece 35½ x 10 x ½ in.
- One piece 29½ x 5¾ x ½ in.

Backboard

Marine plywood

- One piece 35½ x 21¾ x ½ in.

Tray

Marine plywood

- Two pieces 12 x 3 x ½ in.
- Four pieces 3 x 2½ x ½ in.

Spindle

Marine plywood

- One piece 12 x 12 x ½ in.
- One piece 6¾ x 6¾ x ½ in.

Dowel

- Six pieces 4 x ¾ in.

Rack

Marine plywood

- One piece 12 x 4 x ½ in.

- Template on page 124
- Jigsaw
- Drill
- ³⁄₁₆ in. and ⅛ in. drill bits
- Countersink bit
- Wood glue
- Screwdriver

Screws

- 30: 1¼ in.
- 12: 1 in.
- 4: suitable for wall fixings

- Tape measure
- Compasses
- ⅞ in. spade bit
- Filling knife
- Filler
- Sanding block
- 120-grit sandpaper
- Paintbrush
- Exterior primer
- Exterior paint
- Suitable wall fixings

2 Predrill and countersink the following ³⁄₁₆ in. holes ¼ in. in from the edge (unless otherwise stated) of the relevant pieces of marine plywood (see Drilling and Countersinking, page 12).

In the backboard, drill one hole 5 in. from each end of the short sides.

In the roof top, drill one hole 2 in. from each end of the short sides.

In one large (front) tray piece, drill one hole 1 in. from each end of the short sides. Drill one more hole 4 in. from each end and ¾ in. in from one long edge.

In the other large (bottom) tray piece, drill one hole in the short sides, 1 in. from one long side. Drill one more hole 4 in. from each edge and 1 in. from the same long side. On the opposite long side, drill one hole 2 in. from each end.

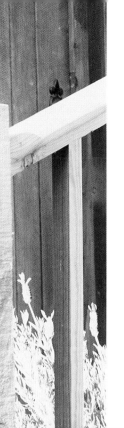

3 Butt the long straight edge of one roof side piece against the end of the backboard. Using a ⅛ in. drill bit, drill pilot holes through the predrilled holes in the backboard into the edges of the side piece. Glue and screw the two pieces together, driving 1¼ in. screws through the predrilled holes into the pilot holes (see Joining Two Pieces with Screws, page 13). Attach the other roof side piece to the other end of the backboard in the same way.

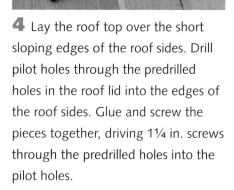

4 Lay the roof top over the short sloping edges of the roof sides. Drill pilot holes through the predrilled holes in the roof lid into the edges of the roof sides. Glue and screw the pieces together, driving 1¼ in. screws through the predrilled holes into the pilot holes.

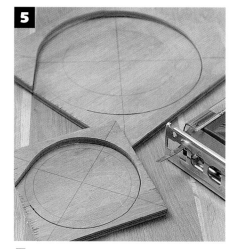

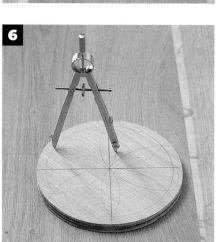

5 Draw diagonals on both spindle pieces of marine plywood to find the center. Using the compasses, draw a 10½ in. diameter circle on the larger piece and a 6 in. diameter circle on the smaller piece. Using a jigsaw, cut out the circles.

6 Mark a 7⅛ in. inner circle on the larger piece. Keeping the compasses at the same measurement, put the point where a diagonal bisects the inner circle and draw an arc. Where the other end of the arc bisects the circle, put the point and draw another arc. Continue all around to make a flower shape with six "petals." Draw a 5⅛ in. circle on the smaller piece and repeat the process.

7 Predrill and countersink a ³⁄₁₆ in. hole at the outer tip of each "petal" on both disks. When drilling the holes, hold the drill at a slight angle, so that the holes slope toward the middle of the small disk and the outer edge of the large disk.

8 Sand both ends of each length of dowel to 15°. The angles at each end must slope in the same direction.

9 Stand one end of a dowel on a drilled hole on the smaller disk, so that the dowel is sloping outward. Drill a pilot hole through the predrilled hole in the disk into the end of the dowel. Glue and screw the pieces together, driving a 1 in. screw through the predrilled hole into the dowel. Attach the remaining five pieces of dowel to the disk in the same way.

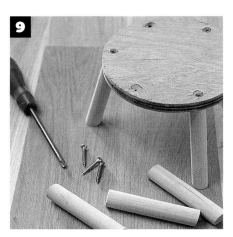

10 Lay the larger disk over the free ends of the dowel, aligning each end with a drilled hole. Attach the disk to the dowel in the same way.

12 Butt one edge of a small tray piece against the end of the tray front piece. Drill pilot holes through the predrilled holes in the large piece into the edge of the small piece. Glue and screw the pieces together, driving 1¼ in. screws through the predrilled holes into the pilot holes. Attach the other small pieces to the large piece in the same way.

11 Using the ⅞ in. spade bit, drill a series of equally spaced holes in the rack piece.

14 Arrange the pieces on the backboard, using the main picture as reference. The precise positions are unimportant as long as there is room to use the elements. Lay the small end of the spindle on the board and draw around it. Remove it and drill three ³⁄₁₆ in. holes within the circle.

13 Lay the tray bottom over the front and sides. Drill pilot holes through the predrilled holes in the bottom piece into the edges of the front and small pieces. Glue and screw the pieces together, driving 1¼ in. screws through the predrilled holes into the pilot holes.

Reposition the spindle, turn the unit over, and drill pilot holes through the drilled holes into the spindle. Glue and screw the pieces together, driving 1¼ in. screws into the pilot holes. Attach the rack and tray to the board using the same principle. Draw a line under the rack, measure up ¼ in., and draw a line, then drill three holes along this line. Draw around the sides and base of the tray, measure in ¼ in., draw lines, and drill two holes on the base line and one on each side line. Glue and screw the rack and tray in place. Fill all screw holes, sand the hose storage, and prime it, then paint it with two coats of exterior paint (see Finishing Techniques, page 110). Drill holes in the corners of the backboard and hang the hose storage on a wall (see Hanging Items on Walls, page 113).

Toolbox

This is a good basic tool kit, though you don't need everything shown here for every project in this book. Before you begin a project, check to make sure that you have all the necessary tools; there's nothing more frustrating than having to stop halfway through a project because you don't have all the equipment.

Invest in a decent-sized toolbox in which to store everything. These boxes are inexpensive and can be found in a variety of sizes.

Finally, take care of your tools. If you keep them clean and free from dust, they will last longer and perform better.

Pencil

Try square

Steel safety ruler

Level

Retractable tape measure

Jigsaw

Rabbeting router bit

Router

Plunge cutter

Countersink bit

Power drill

Hole saw

Spade bit

Straight bit

Chisel

Pin hammer

Claw hammer

Filling knife

Car-body filler

Staple gun

Selection of nails and screws

Flat paintbrush

Pliers

Flathead screwdriver

Crosshead screwdriver

Wood adhesive

Sandpaper in several grades, including wet and dry, with sanding block

Finishing Techniques

A handmade project can be ruined by a poor finish. To give your work a professional look, spend time filling, sanding, and preparing the surfaces before you paint—it will make all the difference.

1 Filling a countersunk screw head

a) The countersunk screw sits with its head a little below the surface of the wood.

b) Fill the countersink with car-body filler. We use this instead of traditional wood filler, which can contract as it dries, leaving you with a dent in the surface. Use a filler knife to smooth the filler into the countersink.

If you are filling a deep hole, it is better to overfill and sand the bump back later. If you try to smooth it flat, you will find that the knife drags the filler out slightly.

c) When dry, simply sand the filler with 120-grit sandpaper. If you do this well, the original hole will be almost undetectable when painted.

2 Filling and sanding an edge

a) The sawed edge of wood, particularly of plywood, is often rough. Use a filler knife to spread car-body filler over the sawed edges. If you are filling a corner, as shown, make sure that the filler covers the joint as well.

b) When the filler is dry, sand the edges with 120-grit sandpaper, and the filler will stay in the splinters and joints, giving a smooth surface.

3 Sealing an edge

If you are going to paint the wood with water-based paint or varnish, then once the edge is smooth, paint it with shellac sanding sealer first. This will keep the wood around the filler from absorbing water from the paint, which would cause it to swell slightly, leaving a depression or crack around the filled hole or joint.

4 Sanding a flat surface

A sanding block is the only way to remove dents and scratches from flat surfaces. If you use sandpaper without a block, it tends to follow the depression, enlarging it rather than removing material from either side to flatten it. There are several types of blocks, although they all do basically the same job.

Sandpaper comes in different grades. In general, rough grades are used first, followed by finer ones to give a completely smooth finish. Wet-and-dry paper is used between coats of paint or varnish, almost polishing the surface, making it completely smooth and removing any trapped dust or flecks of wood and paint. Always finish with a coat of paint or varnish (unless you are distressing a surface), as the action of sanding will affect the finished color.

Keep the block parallel to the surface you are sanding, and on a large surface, move it in small circles to avoid making dents in the wood. We sand pieces smooth with 120-grit sandpaper if they are to be painted,

but give them a final, additional rubdown with 240-grit if they are going to be stained or just varnished.

5 Sanding a rounded edge

Use the same principle as before, but this time angle the sanding block so that it removes the edge of the wood. This is easier if the wood is clamped in place.

6 Sanding a corner

Use the same principle to remove the corners of a piece of wood. Sharp corners and edges will tend to chip and don't hold paint or varnish very well. It is also a good safety precaution to remove corners, especially on low-level items, such as benches.

7 Sanding the inside of a circle

Wrap a length of dowel or pencil in sandpaper to easily work it around the inside diameter of the cut circle. Use the same principle to sand the insides of holes drilled with a spade bit or hole saw.

8 Painting

Always choose a suitable paint for the surface and the treatment it is going to receive. Use woodwork paint, such as satin, and if you use emulsion, always seal it with at least two coats of varnish. Test the varnish on an offcut before painting the whole project, as some varnishes can affect some paint colors.

You can paint the project with a paintbrush, but you may find it easier to achieve a smooth surface—particularly on large flat areas—with a small short-pile roller. Roll the paint on quite thinly and don't roll back and forth over it too much.

Template Techniques

Many of the projects in this book have templates. Enlarge them on a photocopier by the given percentages; the bigger templates will need to be enlarged onto several sheets of paper that must then be taped together. Cut out the templates with scissors.

1 Transferring a template onto wood

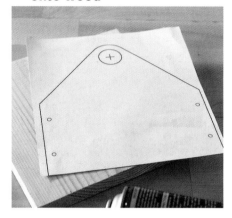

The easiest way to do this is to use spray paper glue (available from stationery and art supply stores) to stick the cutout template onto the wood. However, you may find it clearer to draw around the template and remove it before cutting out the wood; this is what we have done throughout this book. If you do this, then you also have to transfer any marks on the template onto the wood. For screw holes, push a pencil through the X within the circle and mark the wood. Remove the template and draw an X over your mark. For larger shapes, cut them out of the template with scissors, lay the template on the wood, and draw around the shapes.

2 Cutting out shapes

Using a jigsaw, cut around the outer lines on the template or around your drawn lines. On large pieces you may find it easier to cut out the shape roughly first, then go back and cut it out neatly. Cut out curved shapes in sections; where this applies in a project, we have shown the cutout piece surrounded by the offcuts to show you the best way to cut out the pieces.

3 Drilling holes marked on the template

Either drill through the paper and wood, placing the point of the bit on the X within the circle, or mark the wood, as described in Step 1.

4 Screwing two pieces of wood together

This is a very useful technique when you want to cut two identical shapes. Lay the template on the wood first and note any marks. Use 1¼ in. screws to fasten the pieces of wood together, without screwing too close to the outline. Transfer the template onto the wood, and cut out the shapes and drill any holes, as described in Steps 2 and 3. Sand the edges if necessary, then unscrew the pieces of wood to give two identical shapes. Any screw holes can be filled when finishing the project.

If you prefer, you can stick the template onto one of the pieces of wood and then screw the two pieces together. If there are predrill holes marked on the template, drive the screws through those to avoid making unnecessary holes.

Materials

5 Using a router

This is an invaluable technique if you need to produce a number of identical shapes.

a) First cut out the template in thin MDF, using the technique described in Step 2, and sand the edges smooth. Place the template on the wood and draw around it in pencil. Using a jigsaw, cut out the shape roughly, cutting close to the pencil lines, but not within them.

b) Staple the MDF template to the wood, positioning it on the lines. Using a router with a template profiling bit, rout around the template. This bit has a free-spinning wheel that runs along the MDF and a straight cutting edge that cuts the wood to the same line as the template. Remove the template.

MDF

MDF (medium-density fiberboard) is easy to work with and is relatively inexpensive. Its smooth surface is perfect for paint finishes, but it is not waterproof. The dust from cutting MDF can be irritating, so always wear a mask and work in a well-ventilated area.

Lumber

The lumber used in this book is pine, with the exception of the telephone table, and is readily available from home improvement stores. The telephone table is made from beech, though you could use any close-grained hard wood.

Marine plywood

A strong and rigid board made up of layers of wood bonded together with the layers running at right angles to one another and with waterproof glue. Better-quality boards are made up from more and thinner layers of wood, making them more stable.

Suppliers

All the tools and materials used in this book can be bought from home improvement stores or lumber yards. Consult your local telephone directory for outlets near you.

Hanging Items on Walls

There are several projects in this book that have to be hung on a wall—the Bathroom Cabinet and DVD and CD Rack, for example. The instructions with the project tell you that you need suitable wall fixings and screws to go with them. It is impossible to be more precise than this, as walls themselves vary so much.

As long as you know what your wall is made from, your local home improvement center will be able to recommend the fixings and screws you need. If you are unsure as to what your wall is made from, do get professional advice.

Remember that once fully laden, some of the projects will be heavy, so never, never be tempted to use incorrect wall fixings. It is quite possible for an improperly fixed piece to fall off a wall, which will damage it and anything, or anyone, underneath it.

Templates

The percentages given beside each template indicate the percentage by which it must be enlarged to make it the correct size. Measurements are also given to help you check that your enlarged template is the correct size. It is important to double check these measurements on your enlarged template, as not all photocopiers enlarge completely accurately.

The marks on the templates follow this key:

⊕ Holes to be drilled or predrilled

– – – – – – –   Marks to be transferred

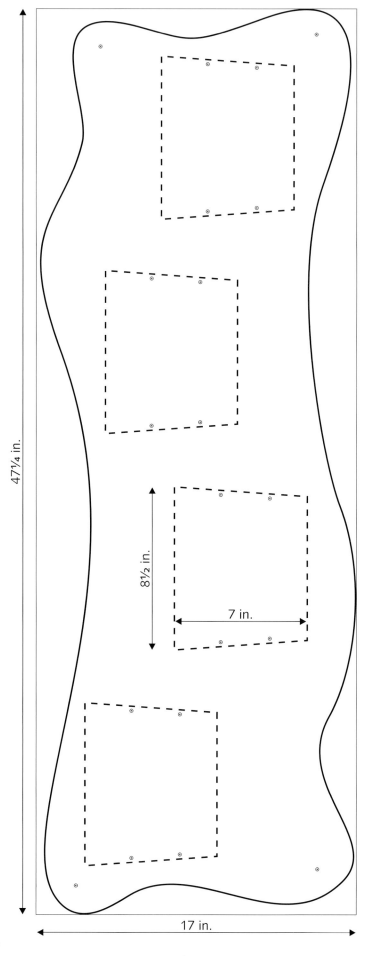

Letter Rack

Page 26

Enlarge by 500 percent.

Hall Seat

Page 36

Enlarge by 667 percent.

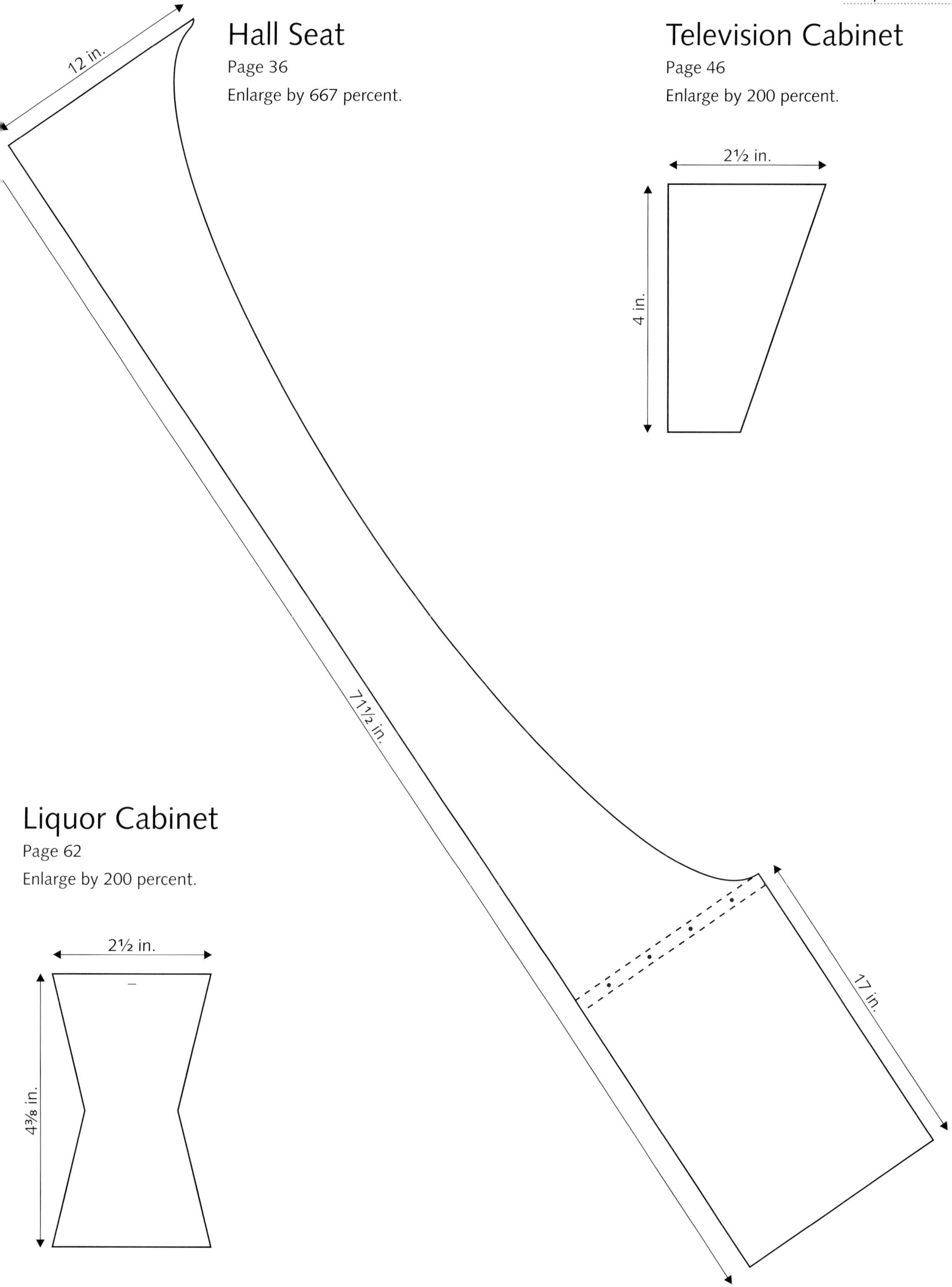

12 in.

71½ in.

Television Cabinet

Page 46

Enlarge by 200 percent.

2½ in.

4 in.

Liquor Cabinet

Page 62

Enlarge by 200 percent.

2½ in.

4³⁄₈ in.

17 in.

Below-Stairs Cupboard

Page 30

This diagram shows how we divided up the space under our staircase and how the cupboards fit into that space. To measure up your staircase, first mark the point on the floor where you want the broom cupboard door to be. Measure from this point to where the stairs meet the floor. Then measure from the marked point to the underside of the stairs. Use a long piece of wood and a level to ensure that you measure the distance absolutely vertically.

Draw these measurements onto a large piece of paper at a scale of 1:10. Connect the ends of the drawn lines to make a triangle. The slope of the triangle will be the angle of your staircase, and this is the angle you must cut the tops of the cupboards to. Measure the width of the stairs to establish the depth of the cupboards: take the measurement underneath the stairs.

Divide up the available space into separate cupboards, bearing in mind the sizes of things you want to store. You must leave approximately ⅜ in. clearance between the sides of the cupboards and the partitions between them.

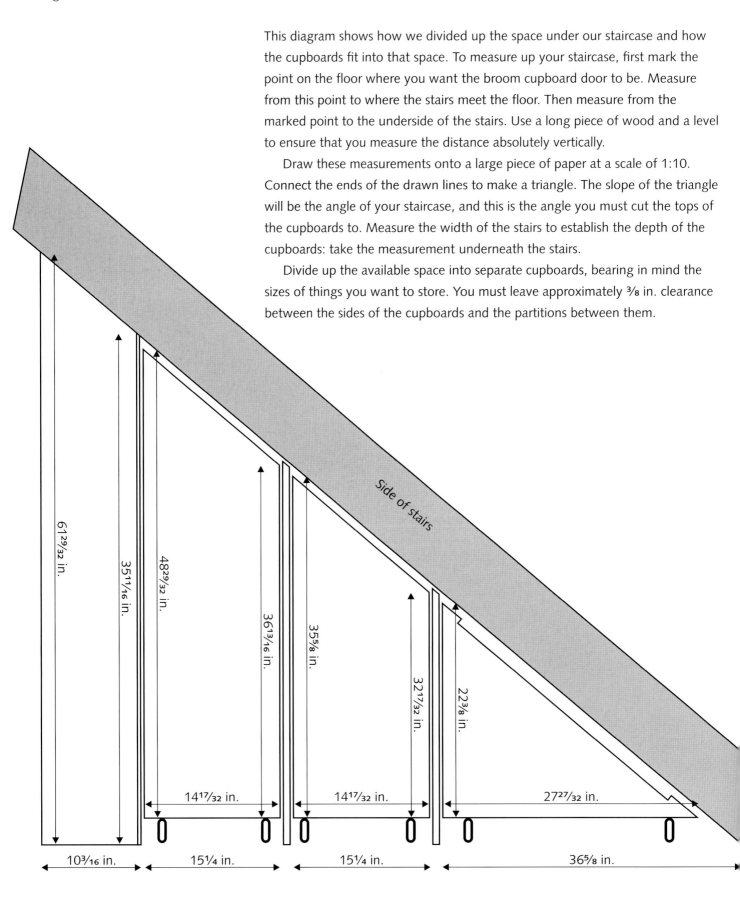

Side of stairs

61²⁹/₃₂ in.

35¹¹/₁₆ in.

48²⁹/₃₂ in.

36¹³/₁₆ in.

35⅝ in.

32¹⁷/₃₂ in.

22⅜ in.

14¹⁷/₃₂ in.

14¹⁷/₃₂ in.

27²⁷/₃₂ in.

10³/₁₆ in.

15¼ in.

15¼ in.

36⅝ in.

Below-Stairs Cupboard

Page 30

Enlarge by 1,000 percent.

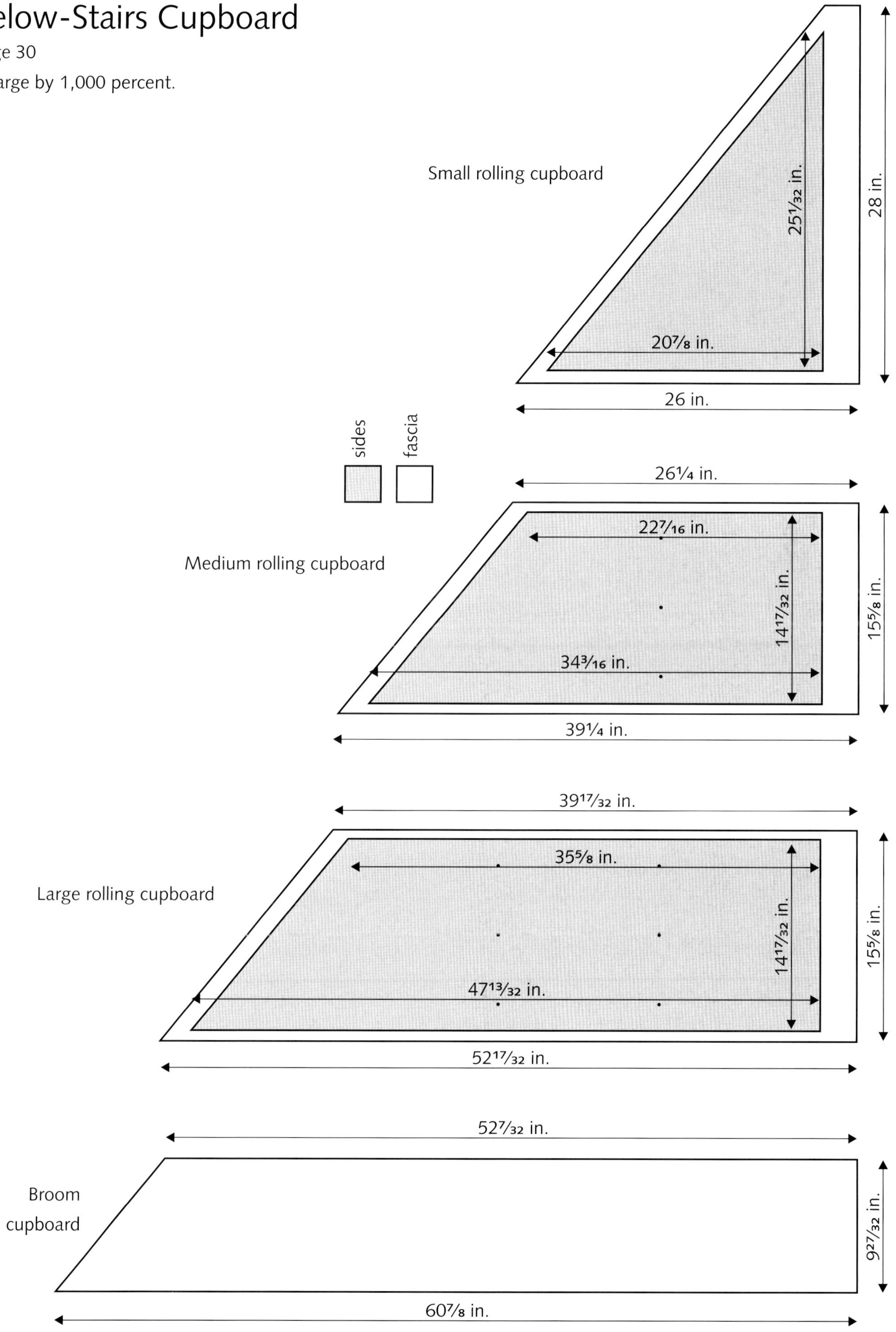

Small rolling cupboard

25¹/₃₂ in.

28 in.

20⁷/₈ in.

26 in.

sides

fascia

Medium rolling cupboard

26¼ in.

22⁷/₁₆ in.

14¹⁷/₃₂ in.

15⁵/₈ in.

34³/₁₆ in.

39¼ in.

Large rolling cupboard

39¹⁷/₃₂ in.

35⁵/₈ in.

14¹⁷/₃₂ in.

15⁵/₈ in.

47¹³/₃₂ in.

52¹⁷/₃₂ in.

Broom
cupboard

52⁷/₃₂ in.

9²⁷/₃₂ in.

60⁷/₈ in.

Floating Shelf

Page 44

Enlarge by 400 percent.

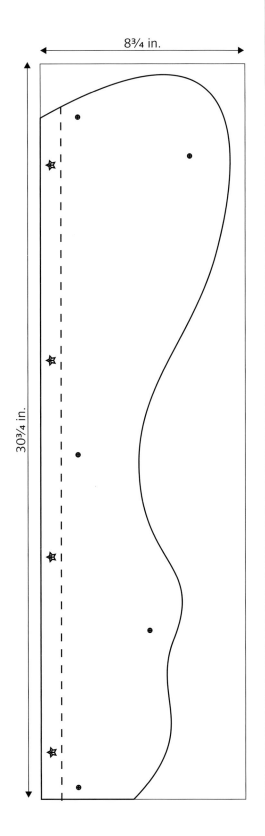

8¾ in.

30¾ in.

DVD and CD Rack

Page 50

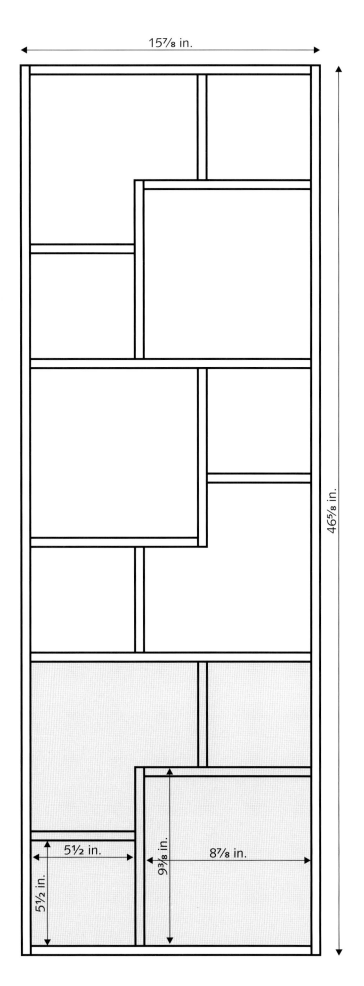

15⅞ in.

46⅝ in.

5½ in.

9⅜ in.

8⅞ in.

5½ in.

Utensil Rack

Page 60

Enlarge by 300 percent.

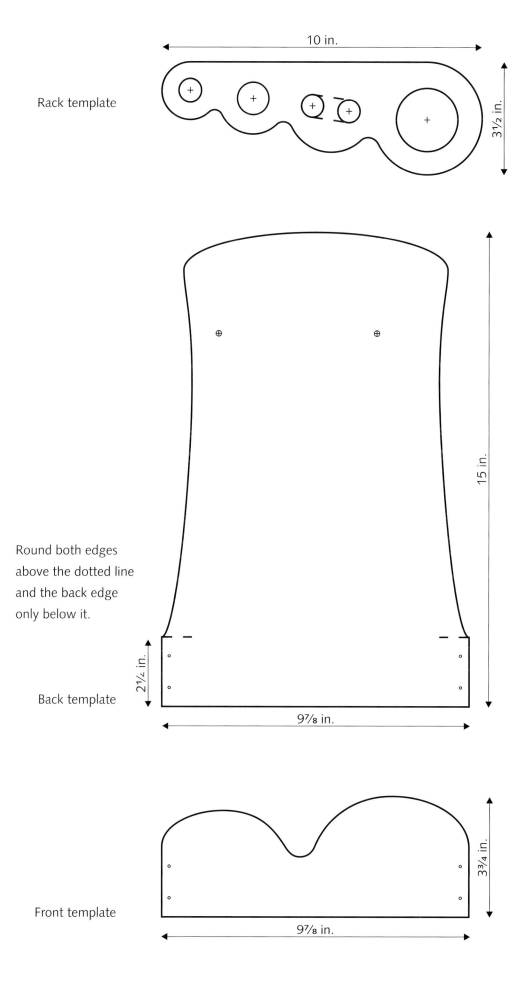

Rack template

10 in.

3½ in.

Round both edges
above the dotted line
and the back edge
only below it.

Back template

2½ in.

15 in.

9⅞ in.

Front template

9⅞ in.

3¾ in.

Nightstand

Page 68 Enlarge by 400 percent.

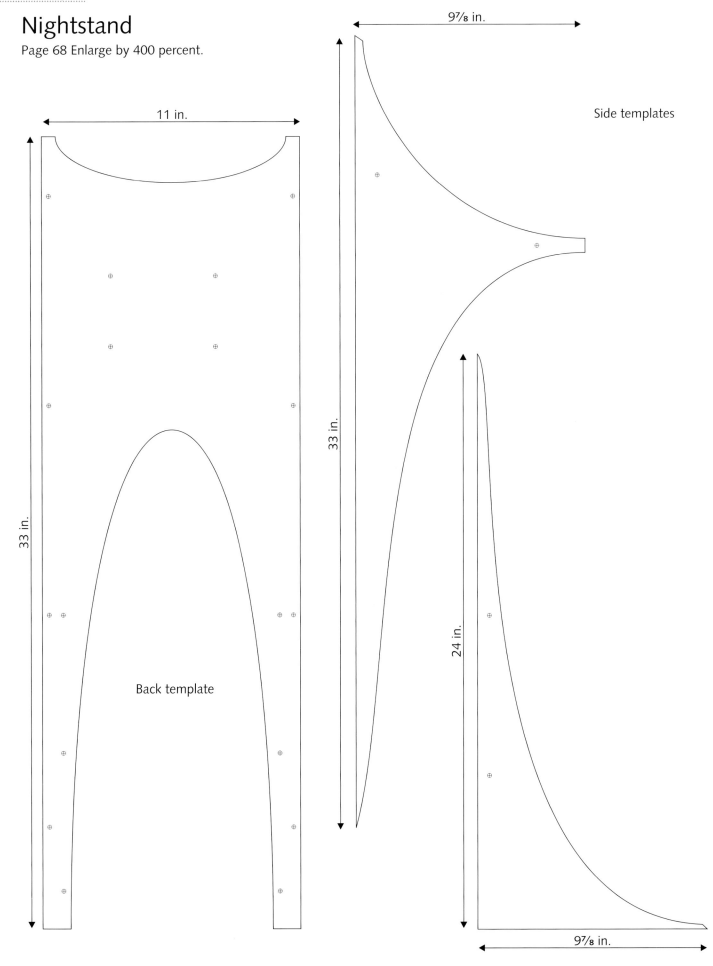

11 in.

33 in.

Back template

9⅞ in.

Side templates

33 in.

24 in.

9⅞ in.

Bathroom Cabinet

Page 82

Enlarge by 333 percent.

12½ in.

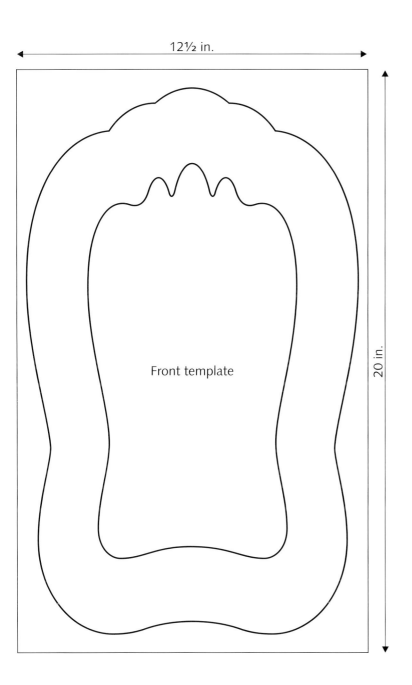

Front template

20 in.

7⅛ in.

23½ in.

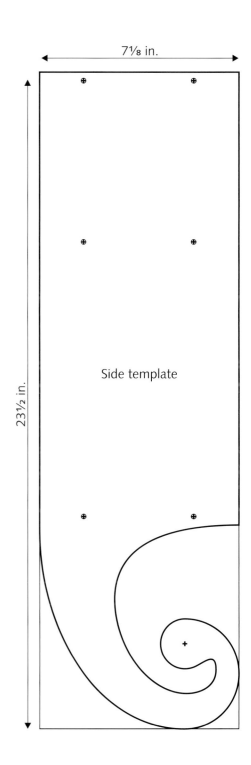

Side template

Mirror with Trays

Page 74

Enlarge by 500 percent.

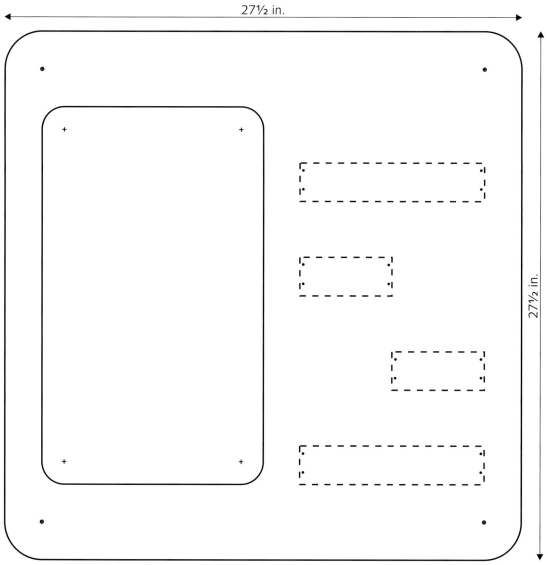

Tipping Drawers

Page 78

Enlarge by 400 percent.

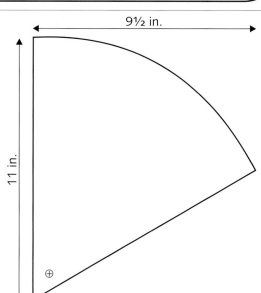

Corner Desk

Page 88

Enlarge by 667 percent

Top template

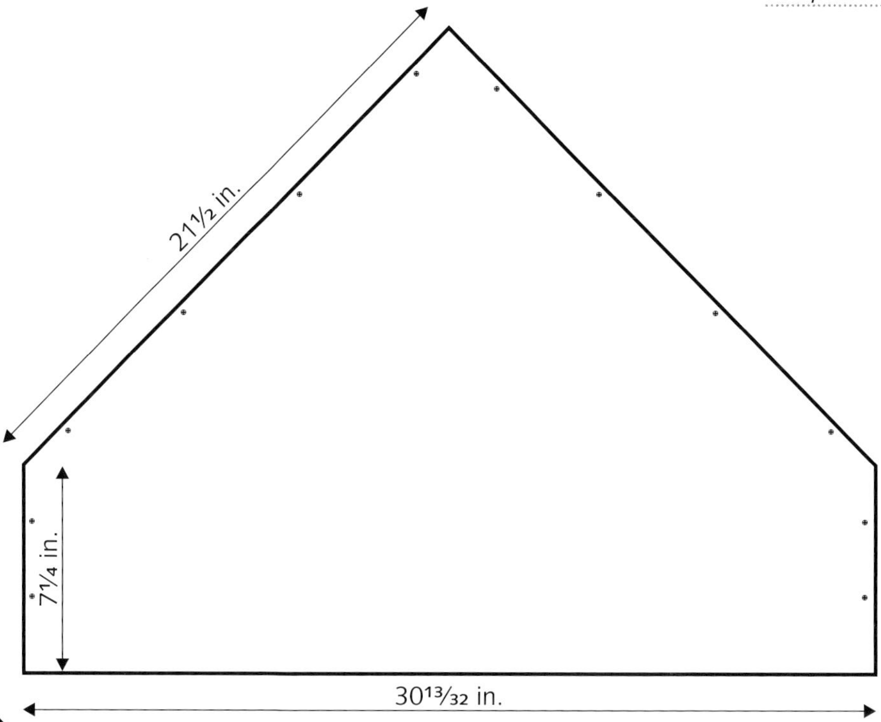

21½ in.

7¼ in.

30¹³/₃₂ in.

Shelf template

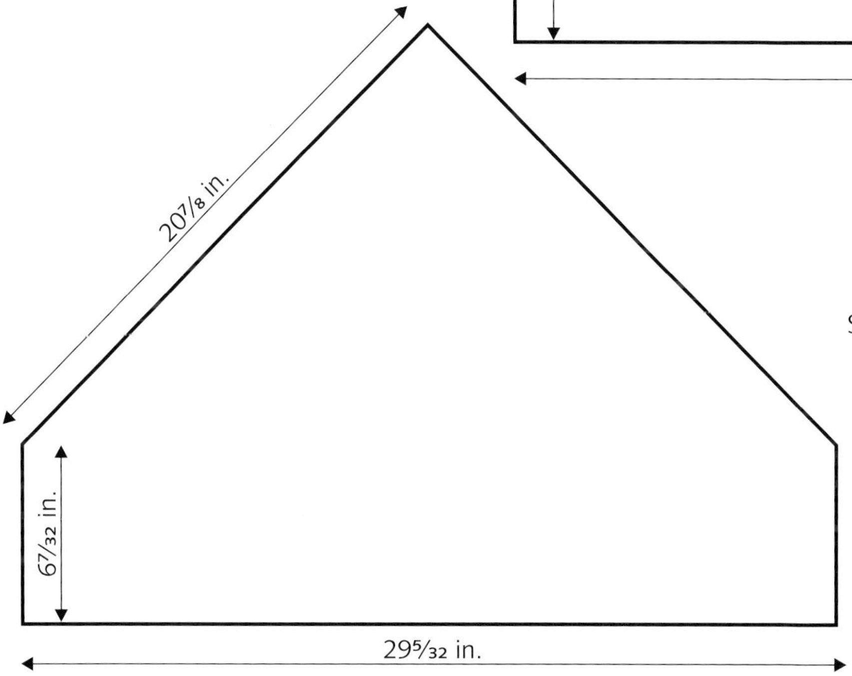

20⅞ in.

6⁷/₃₂ in.

29⁵/₃₂ in.

Base template

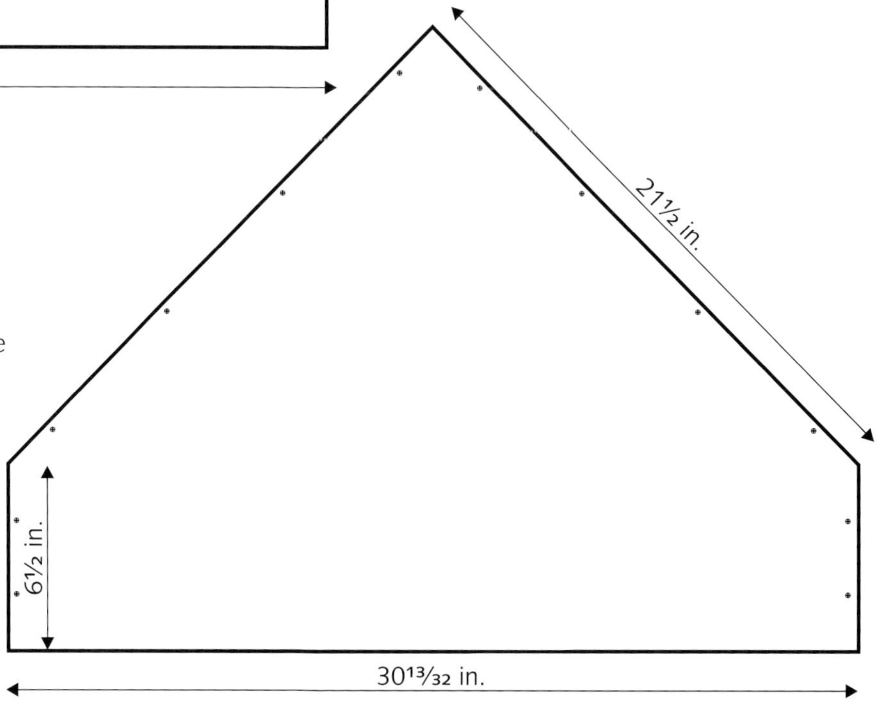

21½ in.

6½ in.

30¹³/₃₂ in.

Workstation Page 96. Enlarge by 714 percent.

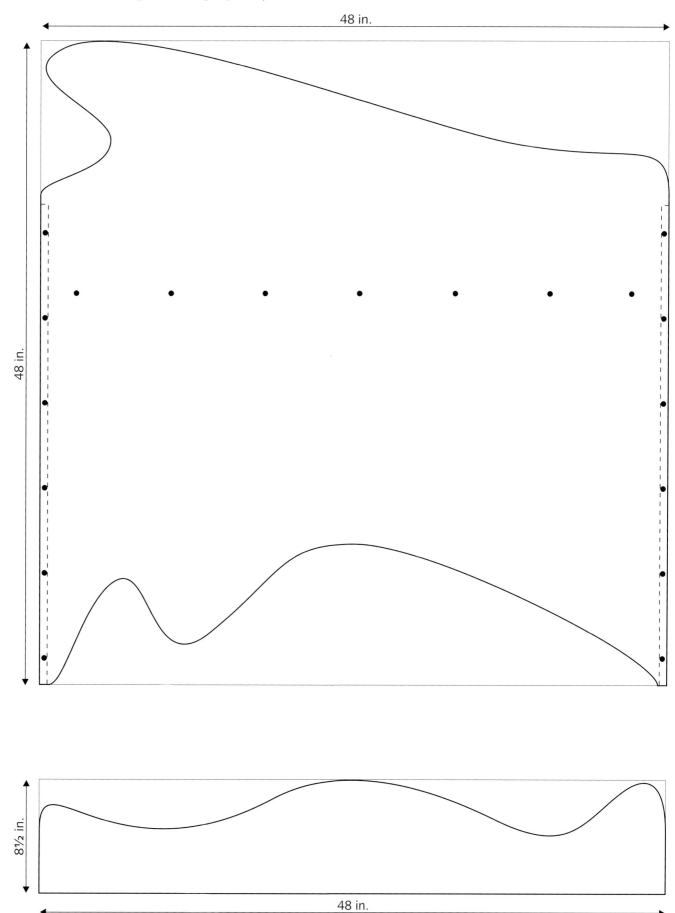

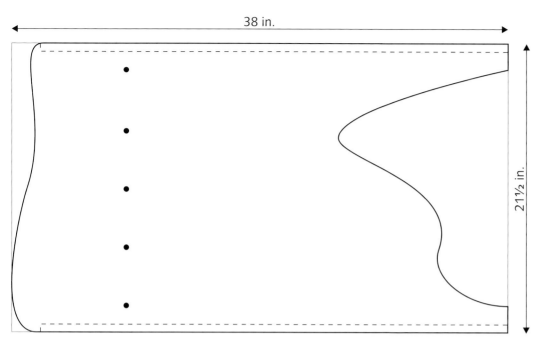

Rout a curve around all the shaped edges of the back, side, and flap pieces of MDF. On the back piece, rout a curve along the sections marked with a dotted line on the side with the countersunk screw holes only. On one side piece, in the section marked with a dotted line, rout a curve along both edges on the right-hand side of the piece. On the other side piece, in the section marked with a dotted line, rout a curve along both edges on the left-hand side of the piece.

Computer Desk Page 92. Enlarge by 667 percent.

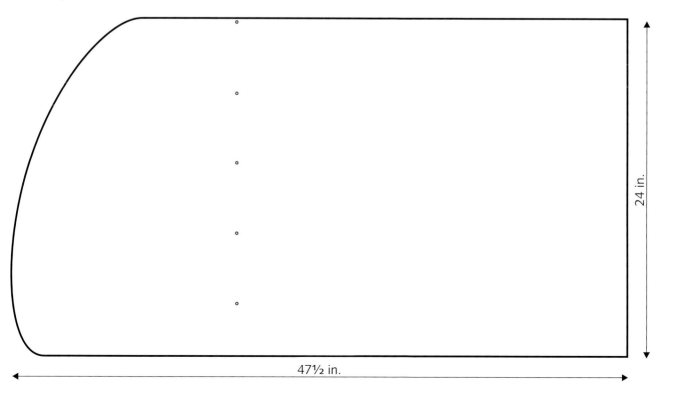

Garden Box

Page 100
Enlarge by 500 percent.

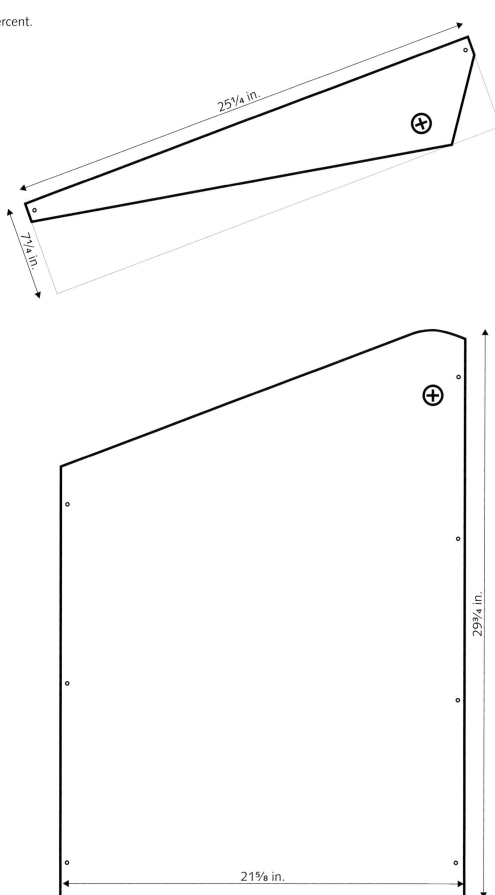

Hose Storage

Page 104

Enlarge by 400 percent.

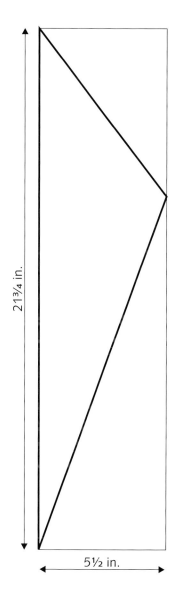

21¾ in.

5½ in.

Safety

It goes without saying that safety is a key issue. Always follow these basic rules and use your common sense. It is never worth the risk of taking shortcuts where safety is concerned.

- Always wear a mask and goggles when cutting wood or MDF, and work in a well-ventilated room if possible.

- When using power tools, follow the manufacturer's instructions carefully; read them through once or twice before you begin. If you feel that you are making a mistake or going off course, simply stop, relax, and start again.

- Keep tools clean and make sure that you use sharp blades and drill bits.

- Never leave a power tool running unattended, even if it's only going to be for a moment. Always turn it off.

- Electrical cords can be dangerous, so keep your eyes open and be careful not to trip over them. This is especially true where extension cords are concerned.

- Wear gloves when handling wire or sharp edges.

- Use adhesives carefully Follow the instructions on the package and make sure that you select the proper glue for the materials that you are working with. If in doubt, ask someone from your local home improvement store.

- Secure items firmly when cutting or drilling.

- Tie long hair back and remove all loose jewelry. Make sure that your clothes don't hang loosely— roll up your sleeves to work.

- Don't be discouraged by these safety pointers; they are here to help you. Most accidents are preventable, so these safety precautions are worth following.

Glossary

Batten A strip of wood, often used to describe wood attached to a wall for holding a component in place.

Bevel Any angle, other than a right angle, cut on a piece of wood or found on a tool blade; to cut such an angle.

Chamfer A small bevel sanded or planed along the edge of a piece of wood to make it less sharp; to sand or plane such a bevel.

Countersink To drill a hole into wood to allow the entire head of a screw or bolt to end up below the surface.

Dowel A short, round length of wood that is fitted into holes in two pieces of wood to hold them together; to fit such a piece of wood.

Dressed all round (DAR) A length of wood or plank that has had all four sides planed before being sold. The dimensions given, however, are for the wood before it was planed, so a DAR length will be smaller than these.

Dressed two sides (D2S) A length of wood or plank that has had two opposing sides planed.

Dry assembling Fitting together or assembling workpieces without fixing or gluing them, to check for an accurate fit and that all angles are true before final fixing.

Grain The direction or alignment of the fibers in a piece of wood.

Hardwood Wood that comes from deciduous, broad-leafed trees—not necessarily harder than softwood.

Jig A device, often homemade, for holding a piece of work in position to enable repeated working to be done.

Marine or waterproof plywood A plywood made with water-resistant hardwood layers and strong glue, used for exterior projects and where moisture and condensation may occur.

Medium-density fiberboard (MDF) A versatile, smooth-surfaced man-made board, produced by binding wood dust together with glue.

Miter A corner joint for which two pieces of wood are cut with bevels of equal angles, usually 45 degrees; to cut such a joint.

Offcut A piece of scrap wood left over after a workpiece has been cut.

Pilot hole A small hole drilled into wood that acts as a guide for the thread of a wood screw.

Primer The first coat of paint on bare wood, designed to seal the surface and provide a base for subsequent coats.

Slat A narrow, usually thin, length of wood used as part of an identical series to form a fence, chair seat, etc.

Softwood Wood that comes from coniferous trees—this is not necessarily softer than hardwood.

Template A pattern or shape, usually drawn on cardboard, paper, or thin board, used as a guide for accurate marking on wood or man-made boards, especially when more than one identical piece is required.

Tongue-and-groove A joint in which a thin tongue of wood on one piece of wood is fitted into a matching groove on another—mainly used in doors and wall panels.

True Describes when something is exact; e.g., a true right angle is perfectly accurate; to smooth perfectly flat with a plane, chisel, or sander.

Acknowledgments

Philip and Kate would like to thank Neil Cameron, Ben Dickens, Lucinda Symons, and Brian Hatton for allowing us to disrupt their homes dreadfully in order to photograph in them.

Much thanks to Lucinda Symons and Brian Hatton for their superb photography and for putting up with wood shavings, chaos, and us. Thanks to Chesca and Kate for good-humored assisting; Denise Brock for excellent styling; and Roger Daniels for inventive page design.

Enormous thanks to Andy Knight for space, access to materials, and time off, without which we couldn't have done this book. Thanks also to his crew for helpful suggestions and lots of encouragement.

Thanks to Cindy Richards and Georgina Harris for commissioning a second book from us.

Thanks to Ore Design (www.oredesign.co.uk) for lending the chair on page 50.